Contents

Preface

In recent years there has been a greatly increased interest in historic gardens of all periods, as well as a desire to renew fine old gardens and landscapes now past their prime, or even derelict. In all too many cases zeal has outrun discretion and much energy has been spent on projects which lack a solid background of information. It is the purpose of this little book to guide the intending restorer or re-creator of period gardens to the essential sources of authentic facts on the design and planting of gardens in Britain from the Norman Conquest to the end of the Georgian era in 1830.

My personal indebtedness in this field is owed to many friends and in particular to members of the Garden History Society. In the first place I must mention the late George Chettle who, soon after his epoch-making excavation of the Great Garden at Kirby Hall in 1935, first aroused my interest in the subject of horticultural restoration. Other archaeologists who have helped me more recently are Mick Aston and Robert Bell, and my personal thanks go to John Anthony, Mrs Mavis Batey, Richard Bisgrove, Dr W. A. Brogden, Mrs Janie Burford, Mrs Mavis Collier, Mrs Maldwin Drummond. Mrs M. Campbell-Culver, Mrs Ruth Duthie, Peter Goodchild, Mrs Jennie Hook, David Jacques, Mark Laird, Dr Sylvia Landsberg, Mrs Hazel Le Rougetel, John Phibbs, Eric Robson, John Sales, Mrs K. Sanecki, Michael Symes and Miss Marion Waller.

Among the corporate bodies to which I wish to express my thanks are Bedfordshire County Council, Cornwall County Council, and Hampshire County Council; the National Trust, the National Trust for Scotland, and the Painshill Park Trust; as well as several county record offices and many libraries including the London Library. Mention must also be made of the help derived from the exhibition 'Historic Gardens in Scotland' (July 1987) produced by Peter McGowan Associates. As often before, I am deeply indebted to Richard Gorer for much assistance on botanical problems of historic identification.

It is impossible to name individually the many persons to whom I am indebted for access to gardens and for information of many kinds: owners, administrators, custodians and, above all, gardeners. To all of them I am truly grateful. Finally I thank my wife, who has visited and discussed many gardens with me, and has read the proofs of this book.

Restoring
Period Gardens

from the Middle Ages
to Georgian Times

John Harvey

2

Printed in Great Britain by C. I. Thomas & Sons (Haverfordwest) Ltd, Press Buildings, Merlins Bridge, Haverfordwest, Dyfed SA61 1XF.

British Library Cataloguing in Publication Data available.

(Cover photograph) The Royal Pavilion, Brighton: John Nash's garden of 1825, in course of restoration in 1987 with temporary seasonal bedding.

(Title page photograph) The Great Garden at Pitmedden, Aberdeenshire, re-created by The National Trust for Scotland.

(Below) The view looking east through the avenue to the park at Erddig, Clwyd. (Photograph: John Harvey.)

Introduction

We are already accustomed to the idea of restoration of buildings and works of art, for the purpose of making their full meaning easier to appreciate and to prolong their life, both for practical and for aesthetic reasons. Methods of conservation and restoration in such cases are applied to complete works already centuries old and which have fallen into decay. It is often asked whether there can be any analogy between such long-lived works and gardens, which by their nature are composed to a great extent of short-lived, even annual, plants.

The answer lies in the principle of renewal: buildings, sculpture, paintings and examples of the minor arts are not themselves eternal; some decay more rapidly than others, according to their materials, the quality of their execution, and the care given, by good fortune or the reverse, to their maintenance. There is, it is true, a fundamental difference between the inert substances of such art and the living material of the plant content of a garden; but every garden is nonetheless an art product and entitled to comparable study and assessment, on its intrinsic merits aesthetically and as an integral part of larger compositions in the same way as decoration, fittings and furniture. In any case some elements of the garden, not only architectural features, but long-lived woody plants, may actually have a longer life than many buildings. Change may be more or less rapid, but is present both in buildings and in gardens and landscapes.

Ever since the excesses of nineteenth-century architects, who sought to return buildings to an earlier hypothetical condition of original design, the very word 'restoration' has been suspect. So far as concerns historic monuments, the term in general modern use is conservation. It is not here necessary to enter into the highly controversial aspects of the borderland between conservation and restoration; it is enough to say that, for garden purposes, the same generally recognized principles should be applied. What these principles are will be discussed later. First it is necessary to answer the question, often put: why restore at all? Is not any attempt at restoration of a former state a denial of progress and of opportunities for contemporary design?

There are several different reasons why restoration in some form may be the most appropriate answer in given cases. Firstly, a garden or landscape may have been created at the same time as the house at its centre, and forms with it a single whole: the survival of both is essential to a full understanding of the intentions of the original patron and the designers who worked for him. In second place there is the garden which, even though it may have lost the house to which it was attached, is of outstanding interest for the quality of its design, for individual features and trees, or as a rare survival of the work of a noted designer. Beyond these two main categories is that concerned with educational value, where restoration of the garden is primarily to provide a living text-book example of a past style.

A further distinction becomes involved when a period garden for purely educational purposes is formed, within a historic site, but without a basis of direct evidence for the former existence of a specific garden just there. In such instances it is proper to describe what is done as a re-creation. While restoration uses all available techniques of research (archaeological, documentary and pictorial) to put back the correct details of a work of art which had actual historical existence, re-creation is admittedly an art of *pastiche,* attempting to provide an impression as accurate as possible, of the type of work which would have been likely at that place in a certain historical period determined to a particular generation.

In both restoration and re-creation it is vitally important that the restraints of serious scholarship should be accepted. At the same time, merely pedantic adherence to former practices may not be effectively possible. This applies especially to the use of materials. It is known, for example, that tunnel-arbours and other supports for vines and climbing plants were formerly made of stakes and wands of hazel, willow or alder, and needed frequent reconstruction as the stakes decayed. In modern economic conditions it would be impractical and self-defeating to follow this traditional method. The use of a metal framework, suitably camouflaged and carrying horizontal wooden wands treated with fungicide, has everything to recommend it. After a few years of growth the plants will conceal the modern material of the framing and future maintenance will be cheaper and much simplified.

Long-term maintenance is one of the chief problems to be faced, since the rate of change in gardens is very fast and the heavy cost of a major restoration may be largely wasted unless a management plan of the work to be done, every year and at longer intervals, is drawn up and strictly followed. It is never possible to eliminate change from a garden, even were this desirable, but it is necessary to envisage an optimum condition to be reached within a certain number of years from planting. Rotas of pruning for trees, of clipping for topiary and edgings, of lifting and re-planting for many bulbs and herbaceous plants, need to be drawn up at the time of design. Probable economies in future finance will have to be faced and may involve curtailment in greater or lesser degree of a programme of restoration. The coat must be cut according to the cloth.

One major factor in maintenance is the degree of public access to the garden restored or re-created. When very large numbers frequent a garden, it is essential to consider the implications in terms of wear and tear, notably on lawns and paths. The re-creation of a small mediaeval *herbarium* with sanded paths, for strictly private use, is in itself simple; yet access for the outside public would demand that the paths should be of compacted gravel (hoggin), of stone flags, or of cobbles or pebbles set in mortar. An alternative method in such a case is to make the relevant section of garden inaccessible but still visible, as has been effectively done at Southampton and at Winchester by Dr Sylvia Landsberg (see Landsberg in Conservation 1984).

In cases of re-creation there is wider scope for choice than in restoration, and it is even possible to form what amounts to a living museum of features, perhaps never found together in a single historical garden but which, nonetheless, combine to give an overall impression not misleading. To achieve such a result it is essential to choose good examples to copy in the case of hard features — paths, fountains, summerhouses, seats or monuments — and to match the forms and varieties of plants as closely as possible. Careful copying by skilled craftsmen of artifacts of wood or stone is not in itself objectionable, and must be accepted as inevitable in re-creation (see Thomas 1984). The restoration of genuine features brings different factors into play.

It is most frequently in regard to plants that serious difficulties are met. In extreme cases the species or forms used at a given period may have been lost to cultivation or even be totally extinct. This is a rare exception and it is usual to be able to find correct species or forms approximating closely to those recorded in paintings or coloured figures of the period. Great care, however, is needed to avoid anachronism, and this applies more particularly to roses. The serious pioneer example of restoration of an ancient garden of 1604 at Edzell Castle, Angus (Tayside), by Dr James Richardson for the Scottish Development Department, loses much of its point through the inclusion of modern floribunda varieties which had no counterpart in the seventeenth century. Similarly the rose garden which forms a beautiful section of the Gilbert White Museum at The Wakes, Selborne, Hampshire, contains many varieties which White could never have seen. Until about 1800 virtually all roses flowered only in June-July, with the exception of the Autumn Damask or so-called Monthly Rose with a scatter of later flowers, and the true Musk Rose which flowers from late July to October. The Musk Rose (*Rosa moschata* Herrm.) is exceptional in another respect: apart from wild brier roses it was the only true climber. Hence it was impossible in mediaeval, Tudor and Stuart times to use roses to cover arbours or pergolas, which were mainly clad with grape-vines and honeysuckles and such native creepers as bindweed and bryony. The Moss Rose was not in Britain until 1724, and most old-fashioned roses are hybrids of the mid nineteenth century, such as Président de Sèze (c. 1835), Souvenir de la Malmaison (1843), Gloire de Dijon (1853), Zephyrine Drouhin (1868) and Mrs John Laing (1887), all of them too late for the periods dealt with in this book (see appendix 2).

The problems raised by fruit and vegetables are considerably more serious. Very few named varieties of fruit can be traced before 1600, and practically all vegetables (though not potherbs and sweet herbs) have been improved almost beyond recognition. In some instances the utilisation of the plant has changed: thus it was not until after 1600 that the Beet became the Beetroot: previously only the leaves had been eaten, cooked in pottage or raw as salad. For about 150 years after the introduction of the Scarlet Runner from America in about 1632 it was grown only as an ornamental climber, but its excellent beans at last came into fashion through Philip Miller's recommendation in his *Gardeners Dictionary*. In spite of the existence since remote times of many edible varieties of the Colewort (*Brassica oleracea*) few of them were known in Britain before 1500. The headed Cabbage, in green and red varieties, seems to have been introduced — or at any rate appreciated — about 1300; the Cauliflower and Broccoli not before the end of the middle ages; Brussels Sprouts not until about 1780.

A factor which lies outside our control is climatic change. We know that, since Roman times, there have been periodic alterations in average temperatures and in rainfall, but there has been a tendency to exaggerate the effects on gardening. It is commonly stated, for example, that our climate in the middle ages was appreciably warmer than it has been in modern times, and that this accounts for the considerable mediaeval production of wine. Although this may have been a contributory factor, the main reasons for giving up large-scale viticulture were rather England's lack of volcanic soils and the consequent mediocre quality of the grapes, and the politico-economic pressure of the trade with Bordeaux after the middle of the twelfth century. The arrival of vintages of real quality from Aquitaine took away from English wines the market which they had enjoyed among the Norman nobility.

It seems that there was a change for the worse in the climate of western Europe early in the fourteenth century, largely responsible for the great famines of 1314 and 1315. From the comments on individual tender plants made later in the century by Friar Henry Daniel (? c 1315-c 1390) it is evident that by 1370-80 the climate was much as it is now. Rosemary could be grown but was liable, then as now, to be killed in severe winters by black frost and north-east winds. Sweet Marjoram and Wall Germander were marginally hardy. The Pomegranate could be grown successfully as a shrub but would not set fruit, as was noted in the seventeenth century and is still true. Subsequent changes, to the new ice age of the seventeenth century with Frost Fairs on the Thames in London, and again to the relative warmth of the later nineteenth and early twentieth century, have involved only slight overall variations. So far as records are available, there is nothing to suggest that the contents of British gardens have been substantially affected by climatic movements.

Changes in our gardens have come mainly as a result of the combination of two factors: the pressure of fashion and the introduction of new sorts of plants. In the course of this book we shall deal in turn with the main periods but something may first be said of the history of conservation and restoration of gardens in Britain. So far as strict restoration of old gardens by replanting is concerned, Britain has not been a pace-setter, and the application of archaeology goes back only to 1935 when the late George Chettle excavated the shaped beds of the Great Garden of Kirby Hall, Northamptonshire, subsequently reconstructed (see Harvey in Conservation 1984). In this respect the way had been shown in the United States of America, where the immense project of Williamsburg, Virginia, had involved excavation of the gardens of the Governor's Palace in 1930-31 (see Hume 1974).

Yet actual restoration had taken place long before at Levens in Westmorland (Cumbria), where the formal garden of topiary had been laid out in 1689 by Guillaume Beaumont, the French head gardener. Maintained by a succession of gardeners, each of whom had trained under his predecessor, for nearly a century after Beaumont's death in 1730, the garden had got out of hand by the time that Alexander Forbes was appointed in 1810. Forbes, the author of *Short Hints on Ornamental Gardening* (Kendal, 1820), carried out an immense replanting of the garden, the park and the estate between 1810 and 1813. It is impossible from the accounts to disentangle those items which relate to the restoration of the formal garden. It may, however, be significant that 25 yews 2 feet (60 centimetres) high were supplied by William Falla of Gateshead in 1811, costing 15 shillings, whereas George Ricketts in 1689 had sent 25 yews from London, price 12s 6d, for the original garden. In 1812 a dozen grafted hollies of different varieties were obtained and 50 tree box costing 12s 6d. Another instance of early replanting of a historic garden was at Chastleton, Oxfordshire, in 1828 and at Drummond Castle in Perthshire (Tayside) a formal garden was made in the 1820s on the site of an earlier one.

Levens was fortunate, not merely in having escaped destruction, but in being restored as a direct result of family tradition and admiration for Beaumont's work. Packwood in Warwickshire was not so lucky. There the hard framework of terraces, with gazebos and a mount, survives intact, but the famous topiary is not a genuine restoration but part of a Victorian replanting of the 1850s. In spite of partial restoration in the 1930s the outcome lacks historical coherence. Another example of the historicism of 1850 is the formal French parterre at Oxburgh Hall in Norfolk, based on a design by Le Blond published in 1709 and restored by the National Trust with variations of planting in the interest of economy of upkeep. A more remarkable instance of Victorian restoration, or re-creation, was the great Queen's Garden to the east of Sudeley Castle, Gloucestershire. In 1855 the estate was inherited by John Coucher Dent, who married Emma Brocklehurst of the Cheshire family. For the rest of her life Mrs Dent's main interest was the reconstruction of this formal garden on the site of the ancient pleasance which had probably been laid out anew for the first visit of Queen Elizabeth I. Although necessarily somewhat simplified in recent years, this remains an impressive example of topiary and knotwork. Such deliberate reconstructions, rare in Britain, were relatively common in Europe and were notably exemplified in the work of Dr Joachim Carvallo at Villandry, Indre-et-Loire, France, in 1906-24 and of Henri Duchêne (1841-1902) and his son Achille (1866-1947) who in 1908 designed the parterre in the east garden of Blenheim Palace, Oxfordshire, as a restoration. In the 1920s Duchêne laid out the water gardens to the west but, although following ideas suggested by Vanbrugh himself, these do not replace features that had historical existence.

Restoration of English historical gardens was given a fresh impetus by Ernest Law (1854-1930), a barrister and historian of Hampton Court Palace (3 volumes, 1885-91). At Hampton Court he designed in 1924 a knot garden in Tudor style, in a sense intended to restore the well documented garden of Henry VIII destroyed under William and Mary. It is worth noting that the Maze, of the end of the seventeenth century, has been continuously maintained and is not a restoration, though it may have replaced an earlier labyrinth of the sixteenth century. Law's design for Elizabethan gardens at New Place, Stratford-on-Avon, Warwickshire, a re-creation laid out in 1919-21, has been considerably changed by subsequent replanting. In a reaction against the 'olde-worlde' exemplified by such Jacobethan gardens, the new profession of landscape architects, whose professional body was founded late in 1929, has generally concentrated upon new design and has tended to discourage restoration and re-creation of gardens of old styles.

In America, at Mount Vernon and Monticello, both in Virginia, serious restoration of Washington's and Jefferson's gardens has been carried out, while at Colonial Williamsburg and elsewhere archaeological investigation has been followed by deliberate re-creation. The strict restoration of greater gardens and landscapes in Europe is exemplified by work in Germany at Klein-Glienicke, Berlin, and at Schwetzingen, Baden-Württemberg, where the parterre was reconstructed in 1974 to its original design. At Eszterháza, County Sopron, Hungary, a total restoration of the immense estate (1764-84) was begun in 1960, and at Het Loo in The Netherlands the Great Garden of 1686-95, which was laid out, like the new Hampton Court, for William and Mary, was scrupulously restored and opened in 1984. In Spain the Royal Botanical Garden in Madrid, founded in 1774, was restored in 1977-82.

The opening of a new period of interest in restoration of gardens in Britain roughly coincided with the founding of the Garden History Society in 1965. Several projects were initiated by the National Trust and by the National Trust for Scotland, such as the formal garden at Moseley Old Hall, Staffordshire, a re-creation by Graham Stuart Thomas (see NT Guide, revised 1986); the major restoration at Westbury Court, Gloucestershire; and re-creations of formal gardens at Edzell Castle and at

Pitmedden, Aberdeenshire (Grampian). Such projects were discussed in papers delivered at the seminar held by the Society at Stowe School on 20th April 1968 and published as its *Occasional Paper No. 1* (1969). In 1970 the Plymouth Barbican Association laid out a series of four small gardens in loosely Elizabethan style. Though not strictly authentic in design or planting, these have great merit as precursors of the movement towards harmonization of gardens with the built environment.

The National Trust in England has, apart from its work on the restoration of smaller formal gardens, adopted a wide policy of replanting of trees in the landscapes for which it is responsible. According to the needs of each case, the nature of the work done varies from normal maintenance and renewal, through restoration, to deliberate re-creation. Where major problems arise, a thorough survey of all trees and identifiable stumps is carried out: the noteworthy report by John Phibbs on the park at Wimpole Hall, Cambridgeshire, made in 1979 and issued by the Trust in 1980, is a model for such surveys (see also John Phibbs, 'An Approach to the Methodology of Recording Historic Landscapes', *Garden History,* XI, 2 [1983] 167-75). Instances of extensive works of research and replanting by the Trust, apart from several to be described later, are Attingham Park, Shropshire; Basildon Park, Berkshire; Dunham Massey, Cheshire; and West Wycombe Park, Buckinghamshire. As a general rule the intention has been to restore the spirit of each design rather than to seek precise accuracy.

In the same spirit there has been work at many private properties, sometimes falling into the category of maintenance rather than that of restoration, as for instance at St Paul's Walden Bury, near Whitwell, Hertfordshire, where the formal layout of c 1725-30 has had continuous existence. In some cases, such as Chiswick Park, Middlesex (London), where an extensive project for restoration is now (1988) being considered, there is diversity of opinion as to which of the several distinct garden designs successively adopted during the eighteenth century should be followed. The complete plan of a grand parterre, visible from the air at Hopetoun House, West Lothian, is unlikely to be restored on account of the very high cost of maintenance. Disappointingly, at another Scottish site, Aberdour Castle, Fife, very thorough archaeological excavation under Gordon Ewart in 1977-80 has failed to reveal any evidence for the former horticultural treatment. The garden, described by a visitor in 1650 as 'so fragrant and delightful that I thought I was still in England', and then perhaps nearly a century old, has left no traces beyond the architectural layout of its hillside terraces, and the only identifiable pollens are of horse chestnut, mulberry and water-lily. A major replanting of the garden took place in 1690-91, and for this there is the complete list of plants supplied by James Sutherland, Keeper of the Physic Garden in Edinburgh (Neil R. Hynd and Gordon Ewart, 'Aberdour Castle Gardens', *Garden History*, XI, 2 [1983] 93-111).

The present book is limited in scope to Britain and in date runs only to 1830, the end of the Georgian period. It is further restricted to deliberate restorations of historical gardens and the re-creation of gardens in authentic style within ancient sites. It is not proposed to deal with schemes of only loosely period character, of which a considerable number have been laid out in recent years. Many projects have taken the form of herb gardens, like those formed at Peterborough and Wells cathedrals and at Michelham Priory in Sussex. Care has generally been taken that the species of plants are correct for the period, but little or no attention has been given to what is known of the details of early design, layout and planting. In the case of Michelham it should be said that there is no suggestion of mediaeval authenticity except in the choice of plants grown, and the design was governed by a primary decision that the garden should be fully accessible to the disabled. The Michelham layout of 1981, by Mrs Virginia Hinze, associating herbs by their medicinal uses, seems to have inspired the much more ambitious garden at Stafford Castle, where it has to be stressed that the planting of many species in the same bed (apart from edgings) has no justification in the sources. Later periods are represented by the fine gardens of the Welsh Folk Museum at St Fagans, Glamorgan, and the beautiful grounds behind Gilbert White's old home at Selborne, Hampshire. Nor has it been possible to make more than passing reference to ancient gardens which have been continually maintained and renewed. The steady replanting of well kept landscapes, especially if in accordance with a properly considered management plan, avoids the need for restoration or for imaginative re-creation.

The book's limitation in terminal date to 1830 is imposed by two historical facts. The first and weightier is that the gardens of the modern age have depended increasingly upon named varieties of plants, relatively few of which survive in trade, even though some are now being rediscovered by painstaking research. It is not possible at present to recover all the nuances of Gardenesque, Victorian and Edwardian gardens, even though the general character of designs by Loudon, Nesfield or Jekyll may be faithfully followed. In second place the character of the documentation available changed dramatically within a few years of 1830. The founding of J. C. Loudon's *Gardener's Magazine* in 1826, followed by Joseph Harrison's *Floricultural Cabinet* in 1833, Joseph Paxton's *Magazine of Botany* in the following year, and of the *Gardener's Chronicle* in 1841 placed firmly on record transient fashions and plans and precise details in abundance. The seal was set within a short time by the application of photography to gardens and to individual plants. To cope with this multiplicity of sources for a century and a half would require more space than the seven centuries which had elapsed between the deaths of Henry I and of George IV.

General principles

For more than a century past discussion, and at times embittered controversy, have surrounded the subject of artistic restoration and in particular that of historic buildings. By now there is a consensus of opinion as to general principles or, at least, preferable attitudes towards the repair and reconstitution of old work. Perhaps the leading principle may be defined in brief as Authenticity: whatever is done should have the authority of knowledge of the original work and its style. In the case of gardens this concerns the plan, details of planting and the plants used. Surviving features and plants should not normally be destroyed unless their replacement, as part of the historical process of maintenance, has become inevitable. In a garden of a single basic date this presents no problem, but what of the garden materially changed at several periods, though without making a clean sweep of its predecessors? (On principles generally, see Sales in Conservation 1984.)

Another major principle, already formulated in regard to the treatment of buildings, has here to be observed: that of historical development. The later changes and accretions to a building or a garden are in themselves part of its interest, leading back to successive generations within a single family, or to new owners. In each instance, of course, a careful assessment must be made of the contributions of each period to the whole, regarded both historically and aesthetically. Considerable weight must be given to the date and style of a surviving house in the garden. For example, where the building contains substantial work of the seventeenth, eighteenth and nineteenth centuries, but with a major refronting of say 1775 still predominant, attention might legitimately be concentrated on surviving trees and features dating from that time and to reconstruction of a layout evidenced by surviving plans, paintings, prints and lists of plants. Considerations of a practical and economic kind play their part: in such a case, the main alternative might be to re-create the Early Victorian gardens with their carpet bedding, now inordinately labour-intensive and hence costly in upkeep. The avoidance of heavy annual expense would here suggest reversion to the earlier and, horticulturally, simpler scheme.

The restoration of gardens of former styles clearly calls for considerable knowledge of the history of gardening, and for an ability to sink modern preconceptions beneath the overall atmosphere of a past era. Owing to the predominant part played in the teaching of landscape architecture by 'design', it is an unfortunate fact that many professionals are positively handicapped by the very qualities which have won them distinction. As with the parallel case of historic buildings, relatively few of the qualified practitioners are able to put off their modern individuality of approach, and hence have great difficulty in making their work harmonize with genuine old remains. Some of the best work achieved has undoubtedly been done not by professionals, but by amateurs of history and research working in close co-operation with gardeners. It is of considerable interest that some of the greatest of the historic gardens were originally created by a like process of collaboration between the owner himself and an endowed chief gardener: Studley Royal, Stourhead, and Mount Edgcumbe are outstanding instances. (See John Harvey, 'The Georgian Garden: Nurseries and Plants' in *The Georgian Group Report and Journal 1986*, 1987, 55-66.)

It cannot be too often or too strongly emphasized that sound restoration, or re-creation, involves the expenditure of a great deal of time. Results cannot be hurried and immense harm can be done by determining a timetable in advance. In many cases the first essential is to arrange for archaeological excavation of the site, or of suitable sections of it. Until the results are known, and have been fully expounded by the archaeologist and digested by the garden restorer, no definite programme of works can be prepared. In the meantime, research of other types must be undertaken to discover all documentary and graphic records of the garden, whether in the form of original archives, early photographs or printed accounts in books and journals. Often it is necessary to carry out fresh work on the family history to establish as much as may be known of the individuals who commissioned a given phase of work, particularly in regard to their marriages and relationships. These can be revealing, both in regard to other patrons of gardening who may have given advice or influenced the original work, and as to sources of record material to be searched for comments and descriptions. The importance of paintings and engravings is obvious, but amateur sketches and watercolours sometimes preserve information never more formally recorded, and precious glimpses of early gardens lurk in the corners and backgrounds of family portraits and conversation pieces.

Even after all this preliminary research has been completed, there may be a lengthy task ahead devoted to the evaluation of what has been found and its conversion into a coherent grouping of hard facts. Only when such a basic assessment has been reached will it be possible to draw up plans for the new planting, based upon lists of likely species drawn up either on a foundation of actual records for that garden or by reasoned deduction from other gardens of similar period and character. In the selection of species to be used, where detailed records of the old planting are not available, care is necessary to ensure that the choice is a likely one for the garden concerned.

Historical accuracy, or at least reasonable probability, can only be attained by considering three different factors, of which one is the date of introduction. If, for example, restoration is to be to an imagined period of 1740, it is obvious that species reaching Britain later than 1739 cannot be used; but further precautions are needed. In the first place, there was always an interval of some years between first introduction and the general availability of a plant in the nursery trade. In practice, ten years should be always assumed unless the garden was of quite exceptional importance, when it is permissible to suppose that new species could be obtained by special favour. Secondly, some assessment must be made of the wealth of the historic owners, for choice rarities commanded so high a price as to be beyond the means of all but a few. Thus, at a time when most ordinary flowering shrubs could be had for 3d or 6d, and roses for 1 shilling each — the new moss rose at 2 shillings being the one exception — a magnolia would be priced at 7s 6d or 15 shillings, an azalea at 7s 6d, a *Rhododendron maximum* at 15 shillings, a camellia 4 shillings. At the same time 100 roots of the Garden Ranunculus, then being grown in many different varieties, would cost from 10 shillings up to £6 according to the age of the varieties included in the order.

The third major factor to be considered is the garden itself: its aspect and soil in particular. Except in the period when large sums were spent on forming deep beds of peat for 'American' gardens of bog plants, particularly of the heather family including azaleas and rhododendrons, calcifuge plants would not have been attempted in areas naturally unsuited to them. Gardeners of earlier times were commonly well informed, reading Gerard, Parkinson and Evelyn during the seventeenth century, and Philip Miller's *Gardeners Dictionary* in its many editions through the eighteenth. The restorer should steep himself in the garden books of the period in the attempt to recapture the outlook of his predecessor in as close detail as possible.

In practice some of the most difficult problems to surmount

arise in old gardens with substantial survivals of their ancient woody planting. If only a few venerable specimens survive in isolation they should be carefully tended and kept in good condition as long as possible. This is not feasible where avenues or clumps survive only in part and gaps require to be filled. There are two main types of solution, of which one has the advantage of very long tradition, namely to patch piecemeal. This is applicable in all cases where there has been some degree of continued maintenance and total restoration is not needed. It was observed by W. H. Matthews in his classic work *Mazes and Labyrinths* that the Hampton Court Maze, originally planted with hornbeam only, had been renewed at various points from time to time so that by 1922 it was a patchwork of privet, hornbeam, yew, holly, hawthorn and sycamore. Matthews remarked that it was 'questionable whether the lack of uniformity ... causes any grief to the bulk of the visitors'.

Principles of sound restoration would insist that future renewals, *as and when actually needed,* should be made in hornbeam, since that was the species employed when the maze was planted. At the end of a lengthy period the hedges would again be entirely of hornbeam as at first. To carry out such partial renewal over many years, in conjunction with regular maintenance, has the advantage that it causes no major disturbance and no heavy expense at one time. There are, nevertheless, two objections which commonly arise. The first is psychological: those responsible for upkeep are anxious to see completed results in short order. Secondly, it is often claimed that it is more economical to raise the money for a total job, by grants or loans, starting afresh with a completely renewed hedge or a clump or avenue replanted after clear felling. Here it can only be said that every case should be considered very carefully on its own merits.

Sometimes it is impossible to restore planting accurately even though there are full records. The most common instance is when a given plant is unobtainable or unusable, as has happened within the past fifteen years with the elm. The ravages of an exceptionally virulent form of Dutch Elm Disease have left few survivors of any form of *Ulmus* beyond hedgerow bushes which, as soon as trunks are formed, become subject to renewed infestation. The substitution of some other tree is unavoidable in replacing avenues or clumps originally planted with elm. The lime is in most cases a suitable substitute and has, for example, been used by Hal Moggridge in replanting the elm avenue at Blenheim, and by the National Trust at Wimpole. The disappearance of old varieties of once fashionable flowers, carnations, primroses, tulips, makes it impossible to produce completely accurate restorations of bedding of the sixteenth to eighteenth centuries, but careful comparison with early paintings and coloured engravings will usually succeed in identifying similar forms.

The fact has to be faced that woody planting, even with mainly long-lived species, has a life of less than three centuries. The age of English Landscape, regarded as a major contribution to world art, began about 1725 and was ending a century later. Thus the great Georgian parks are now mostly over two hundred years old and will at best very shortly reach the end of their natural lives. There is, therefore, a major question to be answered: how far is it possible to perpetuate these magnificent works of art for the enjoyment of future generations? It is a question that needs to be answered almost immediately, and the work resulting from the decision will have to be done within the next twenty-five years. A good deal is in fact already in progress, but financial restraints and conditions of expediency leave room for uncertainty as to the success of some of the restoration being done. There can be little doubt, for instance, that the tendency in favour of clear-felling and total replanting has gone too far, and that more serious efforts to preserve original trees and hedges are required. This is in line with the very proper insistence of architectural conservators upon minimal interference — the principle that new work, carried out *in situ,* should be limited to the least that will ensure safety and effective continuity of use.

There is another advantage in doing work piecemeal whenever possible: minor mistakes can be rectified and the later stages benefit from experience. Just as the original designers and gardeners on the site learned by trial and error, so it is possible for us to put ourselves in a similar attitude towards the restoration of what they did. Every garden or estate bears the stamp of the taste of past owners and of the skill of master gardeners, and we must interpret 'the genius of the place' to incorporate the qualities derived from each individual succession of human personalities. Conservation, restoration and harmonious re-creation all demand a subordination of the modern to the spirit of the old, studied with respect and humility.

The middle ages

1066-1485

For our present purpose only the later middle ages can be considered, as we have no information on the form and content of Anglo-Saxon gardens, and start with the aftermath of the Norman Conquest of 1066. The first specific mention of a pleasure garden relates the visit of William Rufus and his courtiers to Romsey Abbey c 1092 'to look at the roses and other flowering herbs' grown there by the nuns. The end of the period, often placed at the Dissolution of the Monasteries completed in 1540, comes earlier in gardening. In the latter part of the fifteenth century English traditional styles were giving way to the impact of new fashions from Burgundy. As a matter of convenience the final date may be put at 1485, that of the battle of Bosworth, though the influence of Burgundian style on English art, architecture and horticulture had been felt for some years before that.

Unlike the later periods with which we shall deal, the mediaeval is singular in that it yields no surviving examples. Though a few trees, such as yews a thousand years old, do survive, none of them form part of identifiable gardens or designed landscapes. Nor have we any pictures of gardens as they formerly existed earlier than about 1550. Within the scope of the present chapter only a few generalized views of imaginary gardens can be found, indicating style and method in broad terms. Further detail can be derived from documentary research, and the plants used at different dates can be defined, but our knowledge of the planning of gardens is schematic. Only the future exploitation of the resources of excavational archaeology, which in 1935 revealed the seventeenth-century garden of Kirby Hall, and 25 years later that of the first-century Roman palace at Fishbourne in Sussex, can give us precise information.

From what has been said it is evident that all restoration of mediaeval gardens can only be re-creation to an imagined prototype, reconstructed on paper from many different sources. At best, it may be fitted into an overall plan formed by surviving buildings or by stretches of precinct walls. Before attempting to produce a model plan for a garden, thought must be given to the type of garden which it is intended to reproduce. Much depends on size, since the gardens of a manor-house might cover up to several acres and would include orchards of fruit-trees, areas devoted to the main vegetables, and smaller gardens for the cultivation of culinary and medicinal herbs. Separate pleasure gardens might be of substantial size, or else confined to small plots of usually square plan, with a central lawn and surrounding borders of flowers or covered alleys for walking under vines and other climbing plants.

There is no single British text surviving from the middle ages which can be used as a guide to gardening of the period. What we know is a mosaic made up from many sources: fragmentary information derived from royal and other archives, sections of the encyclopaedias of Neckam (late twelfth century) and Bartholomew (mid thirteenth century), the planting list of Henry the Poet (? c 1300), Master Jon Gardener's rhymed treatise of around 1340, Friar Henry Daniel's horticultural asides in his herbals of c 1380, and miscellanea of divers kinds. Even after the information from all native documents has been put together, we depend to a considerable extent upon foreign sources to fill gaps.

Gardens were of several distinct kinds. As at later periods there was a division between the greater areas of parkland with trees planted singly or in rows or copses, and smaller plots of garden in the strict sense. These latter gardens might be for the kitchen only, providing vegetables, potherbs and salads; physic gardens for herbs regarded as curative medicines; pleasure gardens devoted to plants of sweet aroma and perfume and with lovely flowers; or mixed gardens (such as that of Henry the Poet) where plants of different sorts grew together for utility and beauty combined. To some extent, at least, these different types of garden made use of the ground in different ways, involving marked variations of plan.

So far as it is possible to rely on our only mediaeval garden plan, that of the Infirmarer's *herbarium* in Canterbury Cathedral Priory, c 1160-65, medicinal herbs might be planted in straight rows running from east to west across a plot fenced in with diamond trellis. Later, more detailed illustrations from foreign sources suggest that vegetables and potherbs were often grown in long rather narrow beds divided by paths. For ease of access the beds were only some 4 feet (1.20 metres) wide and the paths 2 feet (60 centimetres) or less. Physic gardens, at any rate in the latter part of the period, often consisted of square beds each devoted to a single species, with narrow borders against the surrounding walls. Pleasure gardens were of two quite distinct types. The larger pleasance, which might comprise an acre or more of ground, was frequently surrounded by a moat or by two moats, one inside the other. The narrow strip of land between the two moats was planted with pear trees at the Abbot of Peterborough's new garden in 1302, while the internal space was devoted to beautiful flowering plants of many kinds and probably had a pavilion or summerhouse as in the Pleasance in the Marsh near Kenilworth Castle.

Contrasting with these greater gardens were the small *herbaria* inside the courtyards of castles or alongside manor-houses, intended to be seen from the windows of the upper storey and used for recreation. They included or were surrounded by raised benches of turf, revetted with timber, wickerwork, stone or brick. The turf which formed the seat seems commonly to have incorporated low-growing flowers such as camomile, daisy and trefoil, and was probably covered with cushions except in very dry weather. These small herbers had a square of grass lawn in the centre, sometimes also a fountain and a channel of running water. In later times the place of the fountain was commonly taken by a sundial; but in the twelfth century the *Life of St Godric* describes a vision of a garden at Finchale near Durham, 'laid out on a quadrangular plan, fenced about on all of its four sides by the protection of surrounding hedges. In the midst ... a man ... standing at a reading-desk, well designed and enriched'.

The typical pleasure garden was, however, on a larger scale though basically square in plan and with a central lawn. This was described about 1240 by Bartholomew as 'merry with green trees and herbs'. Bartholomew wrote a more detailed description now lost, but its purport must have been similar to that specified in detail by Albertus Magnus a few years later. The plot was to be levelled, cleared of weeds and covered with rich turf beaten down with wooden mallets. About the lawn in a square were to be planted all sorts of sweet-smelling herbs and beautiful flowers, and between the flower-borders and the central lawn were raised turf benches, with seats also somewhere in the middle of the garden and trees and vines set so as to give shade and at the centre a fountain of water in a stone basin. Continental illuminations show that another form of flower-garden consisted of alternate chequers of grass and bed filling a central space surrounded by a tunnel-arbour supporting vines and climbing plants. In one case we have a list of a hundred kinds of plants grown 25 a side in a square garden planned by the physician and poet Henry English, who seems to have flourished in the later thirteenth and early fourteenth century. The plants are graded from shrubs such as roses and butcher's broom down to low edgings like camomile, periwinkle, strawberries, houseleek and savory. Singularly, vegetables like beet, carrot and parsnip, salads such as lettuce, radish, fenugreek and cress, were mixed with roses, lily, flag iris, violet, columbine and hollyhock, sweet herbs and seasonings like parsley, sage, mint and penny-royal, and a wide range of medicinal herbs. Many of the plants served multiple purposes.

There are no such specific gardens to restore, so that for the mediaeval period it is only possible to re-create examples of the kind of garden which might have been at a particular site. Pioneering in this respect, the Hampshire County Council at the suggestion of the Hampshire Gardens Trust decided to form a garden of period character on the ground to the south of Henry III's Great Hall of Winchester Castle. It is known that there was a small *herbarium* roughly in this position in the thirteenth century, though there was then a wider area which was curtailed by the great Palace designed for Charles II by Sir Christopher Wren. In spite of rather cramped quarters, an attractive and convincing reconstruction was designed by Dr Sylvia Landsberg and adopted after the making of a scale model by Alan Cooper. The garden accurately follows original sources and is planted from an authentic list of what was grown in English gardens down to the death of Queen Eleanor of Castile in 1290, but including also native wild flowers which were certainly being introduced into gardens at the time. Queen Eleanor's Garden was opened by HM Queen Elizabeth the Queen Mother in 1986 and is open free to the public daily.

The garden, like its mediaeval forerunners, is intended to cater for all the senses: the visual beauty of the flowers vies with the aromas of herbs. The chuckle and plash of water in stone channel and fountain charm the ear, along with the cooing of white doves from a loft in the wooden pentice which conceals the modern east wall. Tactile pleasure from the soft turf of the benches or from brushing the taller fragrant herbs can be matched, at least in imagination, by the flavours of figs from the tree and grapes from the vines. The stone fountain, the bronze falcon which surmounts it, and the wooden seat in the garden were all closely copied from, or based on, original works of the thirteenth century still extant in Winchester.

A very different type of garden, of the later middle ages, is being planned by Dr Landsberg for the reconstructed Wealden farmhouse 'Bayleaf' in the Weald and Downland Open Air Museum at Singleton, Sussex. Unlike Queen Eleanor's Garden, this will have a mainly practical basis, including a small orchard of

Queen Eleanor's Garden at Winchester Castle: (above) looking east between the Great Hall on left and the tunnel-arbour. The stone channel for water runs down towards the fountain in the background. (Below) The fountain stands in front of the south doorway of the Great Hall, with stone benches and flower borders. (Photographs: Dr Sylvia Landsberg.)

Queen Eleanor's Garden, Winchester Castle: (above) the Red Rose and the White in flower in the secret garden; (right) roses growing by the tunnel-arbour. (Photographs: John Harvey and Miss K. Bili-kowski.)

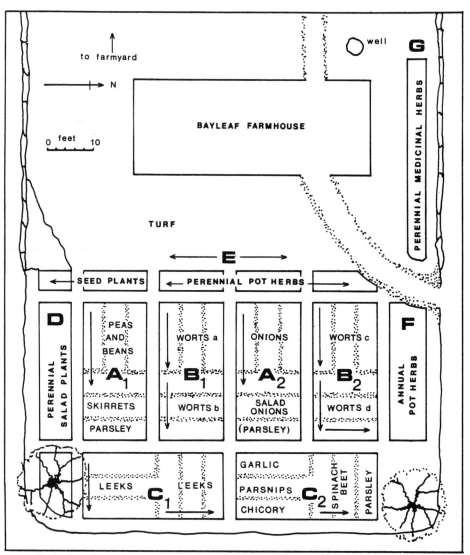

'Bayleaf garden at the Weald and Downland Open Air Museum, Singleton, West Sussex: diagrammatic plan of the garden to show the intended planting for 1988. Crops in the vegetable blocks of beds are to rotate yearly: A_1 and A_2 are replaced by B_1 and B_2; B_1 and B_2 are replaced by C_1 and C_2, and so on. (Copyright design and plan: Dr Sylvia Landsberg.)

*'Bayleaf' farmhouse in May 1987 with the wattled fence of the garden in construction.
(Photograph: Cadbury Lamb.)*

fruit-trees as well as typical beds of herbs and vegetables for the
use of a yeoman's small household.

Tudor gardens

1485-1540

It is impossible to avoid the word 'Tudor' in dealing with periods of English art, including the design of gardens, but the description is fraught with ambiguity. The Tudor dynasty held the throne of England from 1485 to 1603, a period of nearly 120 years, but from an aesthetic standpoint the epoch is almost equally divided into two between late Gothic style and the curious form of early Renaissance known to us as 'Elizabethan'. The sudden change of taste occurred within the reign of Henry VIII, and the crucial date is emphasized by the final Dissolution of the last monasteries in 1540. As an artistic style, Tudor Gothic had set in before the Tudors during the 1470s, when Edward IV on his return from exile in Flanders brought back both foreign artists and continental canons of late Gothic which rapidly dominated the native Perpendicular. In gardening the Flemish influences derived directly from the style practised under the Dukes of Burgundy who had come to rule over the various minor states of the Netherlands, roughly the Benelux countries in modern terms. Though richer and more elaborate than its predecessors, this Burgundian style remained Gothic in all essentials and owed little or nothing to the new cult of the classical antique developed in Italy since the middle of the fourteenth century.

Marks of the style are the use of architecturally designed garden features, notably figures of beasts on the balustrades of staircases and terraces and at the corners of beds and borders, elaborate well-heads and railings and arbours of artistic pretensions. In planting, trees and shrubs were trained into layered 'cake-stand' forms, known as 'estrade' trees, and the use of highly ornamental bowls and vases to contain plants, placed on garden beds, became a general fashion. From about 1460 the cult of the carnation, trained through supporting wicker baskets or horizontal netted grids, almost reached the dimensions of a mania, such as that later felt for the tulip in Turkey and in Holland. Flower-beds of heraldic beasts marked out with strips of lead, or geometrical patterns within squares, took on the name 'knots' which had been given to the formal carved bosses of Gothic vaulting and timbered ceilings. The character of pleasure gardens, however, remained fundamentally what it had been for much of the middle ages. The first 'mounts', deliberately piled up as viewpoints for contemplating the garden within and the park or

The knot, gravel paths and surrounding beds in the garden of Tudor House Museum, Southampton. (Photograph: Hugh Palmer.)

open country outside, began to be made. A few predecessors were probably of accidental formation due to the heaping up of earth at the angles of square moats.

The making of the Mount at New College, Oxford, has been variously put at 1529 and 1594, since the earlier reference in the accounts is not explicit and is now considered more probably to refer to levelling up the area of the garden. Mounds were in fashion by 1540, when John Leland commented on those covered with topiary work climbing corkscrew paths at the castle of the Earl of Northumberland at Wressle in the East Riding of Yorkshire (North Humberside), almost certainly made before the death of the fifth earl in 1527. The great walled garden to the north of Mells Manor House in Somerset was formed for one of the last abbots of Glastonbury soon after 1500, and formerly had internal mounds at its northern angles, looking over raised parapets into the countryside.

So far there has been no attempt to re-create a significant garden of the early Tudor period, though an opportunity may exist at Thornbury Castle in Gloucestershire (Avon). Within the surviving buildings of 1511-22 is the plot in which 'knotts' were laid out in 1520 for the Duke of Buckingham by John Wynde, his chief gardener, and to the east of the castle a larger garden of half an acre, with the great orchard beyond. At Christ Church, Oxford, the remains of the Gothic cloister garth of St Frideswide's Priory, dating from the end of the fifteenth century, now contain a small garden behind a well designed facsimile of the diamond-trellis fence shown in many miniatures of the period. Inside the fence is a border of roses, lilies and other flowers, and on a green lawn are typical raised beds and carnations in ornamental pots. Although there is no historical evidence that gardens were ever placed in the garths of English monastic cloisters, such a garden would probably have existed beside the apartments of abbot or prior. In this case an unhappily derelict space has been converted under the inspiration of Mrs Mavis Batey into an attractive living museum.

1540-1603

With the second part of the Tudor period we enter modern times. It had taken about a century for the new invention of printing to invade all fields of knowledge, and by the accession of Queen Elizabeth I in 1558 the subject of gardening was reached. The first printed book in English on the general practice of horticulture was by Thomas Hill: *A most briefe and plesaunte treatise, teachyng how to dresse, sowe, and set a garden.* In its improved third edition, ten years later, it became *The proffitable arte of gardening* which ran through half a dozen further editions until 1608. At the time of Hill's death, early in the 1570s, he had nearly finished a second and better work, brought out post-humously in 1577 as *The gardeners labyrinth* under the pseudonym of Didymus Mountain. In edition after edition the book continued to be reprinted until 1660. It is from these two books of Hill's, and from their woodcut illustrations, that for the first time we get detailed information on exactly what English gardens were like.

Not only the form of gardens, but their contents, were becoming widely known. The first book to give reasonably accurate information on garden plants known in Britain is *The Names of Herbes,* published by William Turner in 1548. A great deal more information was available after 1570, when the two French botanists Pierre Pena and Matthias de l'Obel (Lobel) brought out in London their great botanical work in Latin, *Stirpium adversaria nova,* which includes much information on plants they had seen on their travels in England. It was not until the last years of the sixteenth century that there appeared in the writings of the surgeon John Gerard what is in effect for the first time a total census of the kinds of plants existing in English gardens. The information comes primarily from Gerard's cata-logue of his own garden in Holborn, where he grew more than a thousand species. The catalogue was twice printed, in 1596 and in 1599, but in 1597 Gerard had published his deservedly famous encyclopaedic work, *The Herball or Generall Historie of Plantes.* Very richly illustrated, this includes virtually all plants then known to European science, but distinguishes those known to the author as growing in Britain.

In many cases the precise identification of the plants presents difficulty, but broadly speaking it is possible to define what could have been the contents of a large English garden at the mid century (from Turner), and in the middle and at the end of Elizabeth's reign (from Pena and Lobel and from Gerard). The *Herball,* with the help of the accurately revised and better illustrated later edition by Thomas Johnson (1633), remains the foundation stone for the historical reconstruction of the English garden flora. It was during the reign of Elizabeth I that the first major wave of introductions of exotic plants had reached Britain. This was largely due to an increasing interest in the pleasure garden filled with flowers. An unexpected by-product of the

Tudor House Museum Garden, Southampton: raised bed with latticed frame supporting carnations. (Photograph: Dr Sylvia Landsberg.)

Reformation was the rivalry between Catholic and Protestant powers to reach an understanding with the Ottoman Empire, leading to embassies and trade missions. A whole new garden flora, of trees, flowering and evergreen shrubs, herbaceous plants and bulbs, was revealed to the West. Furthermore, these plants had in many cases been improved by the skill of Eastern gardeners over several generations. From one species, or perhaps from some forgotten and accidental hybridization, had sprung a myriad of new varieties. This was notably true of the Anemone, Hyacinth, Narcissus, Ranunculus and Tulip, besides the earlier spread of the cultivated double Carnation with its magnificent perfume of cloves. The Cherry Laurel and the Laurustinus, Lilac and Syringa (*Philadelphus*), with various species of Iris and Lily, and the amazing Crown Imperial, were soon followed by many other bulbs including the spring crocus of different colours, a yellow Jasmine to add to the common white, and the most notable of Old World flowering trees, the Horse Chestnut.

The sudden increase in varieties of ornamental plants produced a revolution in the English approach to gardens and gardening, and in particular promoted new professional skills on the part of gardeners and the rise of nurseries. It is probable that Gerard's garden was to some extent exploited by him as a nursery, but he referred intending purchasers of fruit-trees to three nurserymen in the suburbs of London: Henry Banbury of Tothill Street, Westminster, owner of an old business which combined a nursery with osier-growing and basket-making; Mr Warner of Horsleydown in Bermondsey; and Vincent Pointer alias Corbet of Twickenham, a gentleman and father of Richard Corbet who became bishop of Oxford and later of Norwich. All the same, the acquisition of unusual plants in Elizabethan times must to a considerable extent have depended on grace and favour and on acquaintanceship with gardeners of great estates.

One outstanding re-creation of a late Tudor garden has been made, by Dr Sylvia Landsberg, at the Tudor House Museum in Southampton. Though deliberately a collection of features of the time this is a living example of the impact made by effective reconstruction of a past period. In particular the emphasis is on herbal perfumes and aromas, instantly striking the visitor at entry and almost outweighing the visual beauty of the plants in flower. A secret garden on one side, visible through openings in the thick hedge which surmounts a brick wall, includes an original brick beebole of the seventeenth century *in situ,* though the contained straw skep (with its live swarm of bees) is modern. The hum of the bees adds delight to another sense. A central knot garden, based on a guilloche (architectural ornament imitating braided ribbons) pattern found in the woodwork of the Tudor House itself, is carried out in clipped dwarf herbs of four contrasting tones: box, lavender cotton, wall germander and winter savory. Other features of the garden are a stone fountain in its own plot, a rose arbour, a close walk or tunnel under climbers, herb beds, fruit-trees and topiary.

Great care has been taken in the Southampton garden to employ only such varieties and forms of plants as could have been had in England by 1600, and the design and methods of planting are based on contemporary illustrations as far as possible. Among the few debatable questions is the use, as early as 1600, of clipped dwarf box for knots. The plant was certainly available when Gerard wrote in 1597, but it is not mentioned by William Lawson among edging plants in 1617, though it was evidently well known by 1629 when Parkinson published his *Paradisus,* being described as 'of excellent vse to border vp a knot, or the long beds in a Garden'. As a counsel of perfection, until further archaeological

Aerial photograph of the garden of Red Lodge, Bristol, showing the knot. (Photograph: John Anthony.)

or documentary evidence comes to light, it might be preferable to regard the use of clipped dwarf box as a mark of the new style of gardening which came in soon after 1603.

At the knot garden laid out in 1983-85 behind the Red Lodge at Bristol (built c 1590), dwarf box has been used exclusively for the main design, based on a plaster ceiling in the house, though other dwarf herbs of unquestioned authenticity are planted elsewhere in the beds and borders. Even if not strictly contemporary usage — a point by no means certain — this can be excused on the ground of simplicity of upkeep. There is less to be said in favour of the adoption of a strangely mannered design for the tall fence, taken from the French *Maison Rustique* of Charles Estienne and Jean Liebault, not translated into English until 1600 and only popularized by Gervase Markham after 1616. On the other hand, a noteworthy feature of the Bristol garden is its correct placing beneath the upper windows of the house, now a museum of Bristol City Council.

Stuart gardens

1603-1660

In spite of many superficial resemblances between the architecture and minor arts of the Elizabethan and Jacobean periods, the change of dynasty in 1603 coincided with a substantial change of outlook on the part of the greater patrons of the arts in Britain. For over five hundred years England and Scotland had not been simply distinct nations but almost always hostile powers. Under the unassuming but determined sway of James VI and I, the two became welded into Great Britain, one island containing one country and with a single flag of his own devising. Former English isolationism, necessarily defensive against Spain and possible Catholic coalitions of powers, rapidly subsided and was replaced by accommodations with the other leading nations of the West, so that trade and civilized inter-course became the rule rather than the exception. Not merely new plants, but close association with new ideas from France and Italy, rather than from the Netherlands and Germany, exercised an immense impact upon the gardens of Britain. Rightly or wrongly, the seventeenth century opened with a steadily increas-ing emphasis upon scale and magnificence. Courtiers became men of immense wealth, based on international trade, and acquired vast tracts of land which they could afford to turn into parks and wide expanses of gardens. Terraces, grand staircases, lakes and waterworks became essential elements of ostentation.

For the first time there are ample graphic representations of typical gardens of different sizes. Actual scale plans by Robert Smythson and others show exact layouts, and bird's-eye paintings and engravings give precise detail of walls and paths, gateways and balustrades, hedges, fountains and patterned knot gardens and mazes. In some cases field archaeology shows three-dimensional aspects of treatment at some large deserted gardens, never altered or built over but remaining as lines of earthwork. Ranges of terraces and watercourses, pools and canals, can be traced on the ground, as at Holdenby in Northamptonshire and, most notably, in the King's Knot, laid out below Stirling Castle in Scotland for James VI shortly before 1600.

It is in this period, too, that we begin to find quite detailed lists of ornamental plants and seeds acquired by purchase, gift or exchange. Restoration of planting can be provided with a factual basis which is not merely an historian's intelligent surmise. In certain cases it is possible to enumerate the species grown and at times to show exactly where they were planted. Private diaries and journals, as well as accounts, inventories, and other archival records, begin to fill out the horticultural image of the time. We are also entering upon the epoch from which at least a few ancient trees survive as records of planned planting, particularly of the then new fashion of the double row of trees in parallel, or avenue, as at Croft Castle, Herefordshire, where the trees are Sweet Chestnut.

Whereas in the sixteenth century introductions of new plants from abroad had been mainly a by-product of diplomacy and trade, deliberate exploration for plants and the acquisition of new species became aims in their own right. Collections of rare exotics, especially from the Americas, took on special significance as part of the leisure interests of the well-to-do. This was inherent in the development of the pleasure garden, as variety coupled with novelty and rarity was now a major driving impulse. Suitable shelter for tender plants was difficult to provide, so that the principal centre of interest concerned hardy shrubs and herbs from North America, along with new species and varieties from central and northern Europe. By far the most important part in the new search for plants was played by the two John Tradescants, father and son, whose botanical garden at South Lambeth succeeded to Gerard's as the main centre of interest in horticulture. By great good fortune, the Tradescants' records of what plants they grew have survived, in the form of three lists. Building upon the plants in John Parkinson's *Paradisus Terrestris* of 1629, the first English book devoted to ornamental gardens, the elder Tradescant noted, year by year for five years, additional plants not in the book, then in 1634 printed a list of all species then growing in his garden at South Lambeth. In 1656 his son printed a much enlarged list of what was then in the Lambeth garden as an appendix to the catalogue of the family's museum, later to be transported to Oxford as the Ashmolean Collection. This later list gives English as well as Latin names, so that almost every plant can be identified with certainty.

Gaps in our knowledge are filled in by the second great work of Parkinson, his *Theatrum Botanicum* of 1640, and by the first catalogue of plants in the Oxford Botanic Garden, issued in 1648. In spite of doubtful dates for the introduction of several important species, such as the Horse Chestnut, Acacia *(Robinia)* and Cherry Laurel, this is the earliest half-century for which we have almost complete information as to what could have been grown in any decade. The information on planning and design of the greater gardens and their features is also very full, in spite of the disappearance of all the great gardens of the time. The total loss — apart from a few trees — is due largely to the Parliamentary confiscation of royal, ecclesiastical and noble estates after the end of the disastrous Civil War. The year 1650 marks a down beat in our horticultural history.

To some extent the loss of the immense parks of the courtiers is compensated for by increased knowledge of the more modest types of garden. Two books by the Reverend William Lawson, vicar of Ormesby in North Yorkshire from 1583 to his death in 1635, *A New Orchard and Garden* and *The Country House-Wife's Garden,* give us an intimate glimpse into the widespread devotion to gardening of the minor gentry and yeomanry. The books were published in 1617-18, when Lawson claimed to have had more than 48 years of experience in planting, that is since 1570 when he was seventeen: both were many times reprinted and were standard reading for most of the seventeenth century. Between them they covered the orchard, the kitchen garden and the summer garden for flowers, and conveyed all the essential facts needed by the amateur gardener and, for good measure, by the bee-keeper as well.

It was at this time, too, that the importance of planting forest trees was first adequately recognized. The surpassing fame of John Evelyn's *Sylva,* not published until 1664, has tended to overshadow the works of his predecessors in the same field. Arthur Standish brought out two books on the subject, both of which had the royal approval of King James VI and I: *The commons complaint* (1611) and *New directions of experience* (1613). At the same time a forestry surveyor under the Crown, R. Ch. (probably Rocke Church) produced *An olde thrift newly revived* (1612). Slightly earlier was one of the best works on fruit, *The fruiterers secrets* (1604), later reissued as *The husbandmans fruitfull orchard* (1608, 1609), by the mysterious N. F., born in Ireland, of whom nothing else is known. By 1640 England had a substantial literature on all aspects of gardening and planting.

There have so far been no strict restorations of the greater early Stuart gardens, though much of their atmosphere can be felt at Blickling Hall (Norfolk) and, most notably, at Powis Castle, Montgomeryshire (Powys), both in the charge of the National Trust. At Hatfield, Hertfordshire, the gardens begun in 1608 have been in part restored. There, and at the other family seat of the same period at Cranborne, Dorset, the present Marchioness of Salisbury has re-created knot gardens which recall the age of

The Queen's Garden, Kew Palace. The planting is strictly of the 1630s, but the plan is a French design of some fifty years earlier. (Photograph: Cadbury Lamb.)

John Tradescant, first chief gardener to the Cecil Earls of Salisbury. Lady Salisbury has also designed a small knot garden at St Mary's, Lambeth, for the museum of the Tradescant Trust.

The 'Shakespearean' gardens at Stratford-on-Avon, Warwickshire, carried out by Ernest Law in 1919-21, have already been mentioned for their own historic interest, but now have little claim to serious authenticity. A much more direct inspiration for recent restorations is The Queen's Garden behind Kew Palace, designed by Sir George Taylor when Director of the Royal Botanic Gardens and opened by HM Queen Elizabeth II in 1969. The garden is in the style of the Palace (the former 'Dutch House') dated 1631 and built by a London merchant, Samuel Fortrey. The layout and planting are strictly of that period, but the plan chosen for the central parterre is taken from the French gardens at Verneuil as engraved by Du Cerceau over fifty years before the building of the house at Kew.

An English design for a knot garden was used at Moseley Old Hall, Staffordshire, built about 1600 and famous for the clandestine visit of Charles II in 1651. The National Trust in 1963 decided to form a garden such as might then have been seen from the upper windows of the house, and chose one of the designs laid out by the Reverend Walter Stonehouse between 1631 and 1640 at Darfield Rectory in the West Riding of Yorkshire (South Yorkshire). Stonehouse had a most remarkable collection of plants and his own knot was certainly not filled with gravels and stones as at Moseley. Another open knot of dwarf box and gravel, based on a design published by Leonard Meager in 1670, has been made since 1975 at Little Moreton Hall, Cheshire, another property of the Trust (see NT Guide, revised 1986). The use of gravels, intelligible enough as a labour-saving device,

Moseley Old Hall, Staffordshire. The knot is based on a design used by the Reverend Walter Stonehouse at Darfield Rectory. This re-creation uses gravel filling for economy: Stonehouse's beds were filled with a remarkable collection of flowering plants. (Photograph: Cadbury Lamb.)

nevertheless deprives these knot gardens of much of the visual beauty the originals would have possessed.

At Pitmedden, Aberdeenshire (Grampian), the National Trust for Scotland has since 1956 been remaking the Great Garden of Sir Alexander Seton, formed in 1664-75. As a re-creation, however, the garden has been put back a generation by basing the designs of its parterres on those shown at Holyroodhouse in a view of 1647. Dwarf box and coloured pebbles are used, but the overall impression of the garden is heightened by the use of large numbers of bedding plants, costly to replace but worth the expense and effort. At Dunbar's Close in Edinburgh a typical small town garden has been re-created from the designs shown on plans of the city, using gravel paths, box edgings and very simple knots with flowers and dwarf foliage plants. Excavation in 1980 of the garden at Chatelherault near Hamilton, Lanarkshire (Strathclyde), a hunting-lodge of 1732 taken over by the Scottish

Little Moreton Hall, Cheshire: the knot, from a design published in 1670 by Leonard Meager. (Photograph: Cadbury Lamb.)

The Tradescant Garden, designed by the Marchioness of Salisbury, in the churchyard of St Mary's, Lambeth, now the Museum of Garden History.

Development Department in 1979, has revealed the patterns of former parterres which have been marked out in sand in new turf as a temporary measure. Restoration, begun in 1985, is still in progress.

1660-1714

England plunged into open civil war in 1642 and had been transformed into a republican dictatorship by 1650. The effects of this major revolution were paradoxical in their results so far as gardening was concerned. On the one hand, the great country estates, and especially the palatial grounds of the Crown and the bishops, could no longer be maintained and during the 1650s were largely confiscated and to a considerable extent destroyed. On the other hand, not all of the gentry had committed themselves to either side of the political struggle and some were able to carry on sowing and planting unobtrusively. After the end of hostilities they were joined by some of the leaders of the conflict, sadly disillusioned with the peace. Royalists and Parliamentarians in retirement, forgetting their political differences, agreed in exchanging rare plants and bulbs and encouraged the progress of the nursery trade which was just becoming established in the London area and, in a few places, in the provinces.

During the Commonwealth there was, quite apart from traditional gardening interests, an offshoot of the prevailing utilitarian philosophy of the new rulers. The planting of fruit and timber trees, the importation of vegetables and fodder crops from Europe, became articles of policy. The principal figure in this movement was Samuel Hartlib, son of a Polish merchant whose wife was the daughter of an English merchant of Danzig. Hartlib moved to England in 1628 and concerned himself for a time with religious questions but during the Civil War and its aftermath took up the study of agriculture, promoting the methods used in Flanders as an improvement on insular habits. Relations with the Dutch bulb growers became close and it is likely that the London garden trades were much influenced by contacts with the Netherlands from this time onwards.

Before the Restoration of 1660 there had been a noteworthy development, whose significance was not to be realized for almost three hundred years. This was the compilation by Sir Thomas Hanmer, Baronet, of a complete book of gardening based on his own practice at Bettisfield in Flintshire (Clwyd). He included the earliest English gardener's calendar, for 1653, and gave detailed descriptions of all the species of plants, and of many improved varieties, then cultivated by himself and other connoisseurs before 1659. The publication of this book in 1933 (edited by Ivy Elstob, London: Gerald Howe) passed almost unnoticed, but it provides the essential horticultural foundation for restorations

Ham House, Richmond: the view from the central grassed avenue of the Wilderness of hornbeam alleys.

of that period. Far better than the contemporary Tradescant catalogue, it mirrors the actual contents of an individual garden, with instructions for cultivation and minute descriptions of the many sorts of trees, shrubs, fruit, flowering plants and bulbs so greatly cherished by their owner.

Besides Hanmer's book, some of his garden bills survive from the 1650s and 1660s, and other contemporary accounts — particularly those for plants obtained for Kirby Hall — throw further light on the London nursery trade soon after the mid seventeenth century. The catalogue of the younger John Tradescant, printed in his *Musaeum Tradescantianum* of 1656, provides an authoritative list of the garden plants available just before the Restoration of 1660. Soon after the Restoration new gardens were begun and records proliferate, both in the form of surviving accounts and (from 1677) seedsmen's and nurserymen's lists. Gardening books of importance began to issue from the press, notably John Rea's *Flora* of 1664-5, which was followed by *The florist's vade-mecum* (1682) written by Rea's son-in-law Samuel Gilbert. *The English gardener* by Leonard Meager (1670) was a highly practical work, and so was John Worlidge's *Systema horti-culturae: or, the art of gardening* (1677). At Edinburgh in 1683 was published *The Scots gard'ner* by John Reid, the first of its kind north of the Border. There were also many specialized books on the growing of fruit-trees, forest trees and vines.

Ham House, Richmond: the parterre, with period planting faithfully reproduced.

Several major restorations have taken place at gardens belonging to this period. Especially important is what has been done at Ham House near Richmond, Surrey (London). There the gardens were splendidly laid out between 1671 and 1679, but work went on later as surviving accounts show that in November 1693 an order of 150 Pyracantha, 60 Laurustinus and six Spanish Broom was planted, as well as 64 Mezereons, 20 Althaea frutex (*Hibiscus syriacus*), 50 White Jessamine, 26 Honeysuckles and very large numbers of flowering plants: Carnations, Hollyhocks, Double Sweet Rockets and annuals such as Larkspur, African Marigolds, Candytuft and Nasturtiums (*Tropaeolum*). A parterre to the east of the house and the wilderness to the south beyond lawns and gravel walks have been reconstructed by the National Trust since 1978 after a period of detailed research and the construction of a scale model by Miss Lucy Henderson in 1974.

At Kirby Hall, Northamptonshire, the Great Garden, found by excavation in 1935, has been restored in form, though not with authentic planting, by the Department of the Environment. In the light of much research in the extensive documentary sources it is hoped that there may be replanting of the Privy Garden on the south side of the house, where many choice plants were grown between 1685 and 1706.

Ham House, Richmond: the walk surrounding the parterre, of clipped yew shaded by standard hornbeams.
Kirby Hall, Northamptonshire: aerial view of the house and Great Garden, restored from the excavated finds of 1935. The site of the Privy Garden lies beyond, to right of the house. (Copyright: Cambridge University Collection.)

Hampton Court, with its Maze, has already been mentioned, as well as Ernest Law's knot garden of 1924. An extremely important work of scholarly restoration following detailed survey and research was carried out in 1987 in replanting the limes by the semicircular canal. This is a victory for authenticity in that, on the advice of the Garden History Society, the original species *(Tilia x europaea / x vulgaris)* has been used after lengthy discussion. Public controversy had been aroused by the proposal to fell the few original trees, which would not at best have survived much longer, but expert opinion was seriously divided as to whether a different, and supposedly superior, form of modern lime ought not to be substituted for the old. What is to be regretted on historical grounds is that it was not regarded as feasible to wait some years for new saplings to be propagated from the original clone, which was minutely different from the continental stock of trees now planted. The survey and the recent replanting at Hampton Court are due to David Jacques.

In some ways the most striking of all the works of this type effected in the past twenty years is the complete rehabilitation of the forgotten gardens of Westbury Court in Gloucestershire, originally dating from 1696-1705, with additions of c 1715. The property passed to the National Trust in 1967, but Irvine Gray had already for some years been studying the surviving documents and lectured on them to the Garden History Society on 27th April 1968 (published in the Society's *Occasional Paper No. 1* in 1969). The restoration of the garden in its initial form, though with some simplifications, had been completed by the summer of 1973, but much has been done since then. Owing to the loss of that part of the original garden which lay north of the Long Canal, it was not possible simply to follow the details shown in Kip's view of c 1707, but the parterre has been re-created on its old plan beyond the T-Canal to the south. In all essentials Westbury provides the perfect model for both restoration and re-creation (see NT Guide, revised 1986, with plant and fruit lists).

The far larger grounds at Wrest Park, Bedfordshire, belong mainly to 1706-11, with relatively slight changes by Capability Brown c 1758-60 and rebuilding of the house on a new site in 1834-9. This has involved the re-creation of formal gardens to the north of their old position, and buildings of various dates are included such as the Bowling Green House of 1735, the Orangery and Nursery Garden of 1836 and the Chinese Bridge of 1874-6. Restoration of the buildings and monuments has continued over

Westbury Court Garden, Westbury-on-Severn, Gloucestershire: the Long Canal, looking towards the Tall Pavilion. (Photograph: Cadbury Lamb.)

many years under the Ancient Monuments Branch of the Ministry of Works and its successors, and more recently there has been re-creation of the gardens in harmony with the original design. The fact that Wrest Park contains works of many successive periods has inevitably meant that compromises with authenticity have had to be made, but in fundamentals it remains the finest living example in Britain of the school of Le Nôtre and Versailles, saved from banality by Thomas Archer's Baroque pavilion of 1711-12, set at the end of the Long Water.

Westbury Court Garden: the Gazebo with the terrace and T-canal. (Photograph: Cadbury Lamb.)

Westbury Court Garden: the Parterre as re-created. (Photograph: Cadbury Lamb.)

Wrest Park, Bedfordshire: the Long Water looking towards Thomas Archer's pavilion of 1711-12.

Early Georgian gardens

1714-1760

During the last years of Charles II the French style of gardening on a grand scale, as practised by André Le Nôtre at Versailles, had set the tone of the greater English estates. Strict formality and the planting of grand avenues, sometimes several miles long, became the norm, and this was coupled with rigidly planned parterres for the flower garden. Modified by the more intimate, but still extremely formal, Dutch style under William III, gardens tended to become dominated by evergreens, especially in the form of clipped topiary. Continuing through the reign of Queen Anne, this carried on in smaller gardens almost to the end of the eighteenth century and the style ruled fashionable taste long after it had first been ridiculed by Addison in 1712. It was only after the accession of George I that a softening of the scene began to be noticeable, perhaps first at Studley Royal in Yorkshire (North Yorkshire), though efforts to introduce asymmetry had taken place earlier.

The death of Queen Anne, last of the Stuarts, on 1st August 1714, marked the close of an era, but it was also the end of a significant generation of horticulturists. One year earlier had died Henry Compton, Bishop of London, a central figure in the new age of plantsmanship which had followed the Restoration. Compton's collector, the missionary clergyman John Banister, active in Virginia from 1678, was the most significant introducer of plants from America after the Tradescants, and the bishop's grounds at Fulham Palace became the first British arboretum. Another key personality also had disappeared from the scene: George London, the dominant partner in the Brompton Park Nursery since 1689, died on 12th January 1714. Apart from his commanding position in the nursery trade, London had been chief gardener to Bishop Compton at Fulham for over thirty years and was the principal adviser to the Duchess of Beaufort in her far-reaching horticultural activity at Badminton. With the death of Louis XIV in 1715, the mainspring of the formal style was broken and European gardening turned a new page, soon to be filled by the exploits of another generation of English gardeners.

The fascination of the first half of the eighteenth century is that, though still largely under the sway of the grandiose and the architectural, successive waves of increasing naturalism steadily moved on towards the later creation of the school of English Landscape, by some regarded as this country's greatest contribution to art on an international level. To an unusual extent, the restoration of gardens of 1715-60 will depend upon the facts of each individual case and no general rules can be laid down. It was a time of rapidly increasing stocks of new plants, particularly those brought from the British colonies in North America, mostly hardy. Since many of these new species were flowering trees and shrubs or herbaceous plants suitable for beds and borders, the contents of the nurseries played a large part in superseding the older reliance on evergreens. The reign of Brompton Park had ended with the death of London in 1714 and the retirement of his partner Henry Wise. Their successors soon lost the confidence of their customers and the Kensington Gore nursery of Robert Furber, just opposite the gates of the palace, became the main centre for the burgeoning trade. Furber's grounds were already noted by 1716, and he was issuing important catalogues by 1724, when that of his trees and shrubs was reprinted by Philip Miller. Copies of Furber's lists of trees and shrubs, and of fruit-trees, the first known in book form in Britain, survive for 1727, and his famous illustrated work *Twelve Months of Flowers* of 1730 was in effect the first illustrated nurseryman's catalogue (see appendix 1). Flowering plants were again in fashion: Batty Langley advocated perfumed flowers 'in every walk', and Richard Bateman and Philip Southcote began planting. Miller's larger *Gardeners Dictionary* in 1731 superseded his book of 1724 and remained the standard horticultural work in general use for the rest of the century. For Scotland James Justice published *The Scots Gardener's Directory* in 1754.

The nursery trade was affected in another way by the fading reputation of Brompton Park. Dissatisfaction with its high prices, added to costly transportation, had already led to the founding of nurseries in the remoter parts of England and in southern Scotland. As these provincial firms built up their stock, they were able within a few years to show that they were effective as sources of supply for all but the most expensive of recent introductions. The first of the really big nurseries outside the London area were those at York, where the Friars' Gardens was certainly a nursery from 1695 and becoming influential by 1715, and at Pontefract, where the nursery trade grew out of liquorice growing as in Westminster it had done from osier beds and basket-weaving. The first of the greater Scottish nurseries was that of John McAslan at Glasgow, founded in 1717, and the second, Robert Dickson's at Hassendeanburn near Hawick, Roxburghshire (Borders), of 1728. At Hebburn Quay near Gateshead, Durham

Studley Royal, North Yorkshire: the Moon Lake and Temple, embowered in woodland. (Photograph: Cadbury Lamb.)

(Tyne and Wear) a nursery started in 1734 that was destined fifty years later to become the largest of all British tree nurseries under the family of Falla. Other firms were soon set up in the Midlands, as at Newark, Nottinghamshire, by 1720, the same year that William Lucombe set up the first West of England nursery at Exeter. This spread of the plant trade across the country led directly to an increased interest in ornamental gardening among those not in the categories of nobility or the upper gentry, and so within a few years brought the prices of most plants down within the reach of almost everybody.

As has been said already, it was at Studley Royal that a new wave of design began about 1715. The immense estate, which came to include the ruins of Fountains Abbey, comprises work of two main periods: the formation of Studley for John Aislabie from 1715 onwards under his gardener William Fisher, and its expansion into the adjoining Fountains precinct after it had been bought by John's son William Aislabie in 1768. After a long period of decline the whole property was purchased in 1966 by the West Riding County Council, and the wise policy of restoration followed subsequently is largely due to Mr W. T. C. Walker, that council's Deputy Architect (see Exhibition Catalogue, 'Mr Aislabie's Gardens', Bradford: New Arcadians, 1981).

Claremont, Surrey: the Amphitheatre designed by Charles Bridgeman seen from across the lake. (Photograph: John Harvey.)

The estate passed to the National Trust in 1983.

An important part of the contemporary grounds of Claremont, Surrey, had come to the National Trust in 1950 and since 1975 has been extensively cleared and restored under the general direction of Graham Stuart Thomas. The most dramatic work is the revelation of the amphitheatre, opened up by 1977, from overgrowth which had obscured its very existence. Designed by Charles Bridgeman soon after 1715, this was only one of a succession of major features on the estate which had first been planted under Vanbrugh and was later to have work done by Kent and by Brown (see NT Guide, 1984). The next example, chronologically, is the large-scale restoration of the grounds at Erddig in Denbighshire (Clwyd), also under the National Trust. The gardens, almost entirely of 1718-32, had disappeared or were heavily overgrown. The problem of dealing with the trees, most of them long past their prime, has had to be dealt with by drastic felling and replanting. Owing to the extreme conservatism of the Yorke family over more than two centuries, and their rich accumulation of records, it was possible to carry out a total reconstruction of the garden by the time the property was opened to the public in 1977. Though largely original, what has been restored includes also Victorian and Edwardian features (see NT

Claremont, Surrey: looking north-east from the Bowling Green to Vanbrugh's belvedere of 1715.

Guide, revised 1987).

Wroxton Abbey, Oxfordshire, near Banbury, has a complex horticultural history. The house was built in 1618-31 but the earliest work on the present gardens was of 1727-32 by Tilleman Bobart from Oxford, whose cross-walk and terraces survive. Under the advice of Sanderson Miller, Bobart's formal layout was grassed over and a 'rococo' landscape and water gardens were formed after 1735. The estate was bought by Fairleigh Dickinson University of New Jersey, USA, in 1963, and renamed Wroxton College. From 1978 an extensive programme of restoration and reconstruction has been in progress under Paul Edwards. In particular the Grand and Little Cascades below the Great Pond have been reinstated, and since 1983 work has moved on to the Victorian flower gardens (see Edwards in Conservation 1984). Another landscape on which Paul Edwards is working, of the same rococo period (c 1738-48) is at Painswick House, Gloucestershire. The garden as it was in 1748 was painted by Thomas Robins the Elder in exquisite detail, so that there is a complete visual basis for restoration. Five of the 21 garden buildings have survived as well as other features including a statue of Pan. Work began in 1984 and major clearance has since been done.

Mention must be made of the gigantic landscape at Stowe, Buckinghamshire, with several groups of features of different dates, from Bridgeman in the 1720s and 1730s, through Kent and Brown, who was chief gardener in 1741-51, to the last quarter of the eighteenth century. Largely owing to the enthusiasm and wide researches of George Clarke, serious rehabilitation of the temples and features was begun in 1965 under Hugh Creighton as architect, and a programme for the woodland plantings was drawn up in 1967 by John Workman, Forestry Adviser to the National Trust. Hitherto inadequate funds, and the use of the estate as a public school, have precluded any full restoration of the vast area involved, but work proceeds on the basic principle of restoration to the overall condition of 1800, after the last of the main campaigns of original work.

Painshill Park in Walton-on-Thames, Surrey, must take pride of place in any consideration of garden restorations of the present time. Although the area in question (160 acres; 65 ha) is only about three-quarters of the original park and pleasure grounds, it includes the sites of all the important features of the landscape planted by the Honourable Charles Hamilton between 1738 and

The formal replanting of the Yew Alley at Erddig, Clwyd; note old variegated holly on the right.

Painshill Park, Surrey: (left) perspective drawing by Mark Laird of the Amphitheatre with the Gothic Temple beyond. (Below) drawing by Mark Laird to show the effect of the restored planting after five to seven years. (Copyright drawings: Mark Laird.)

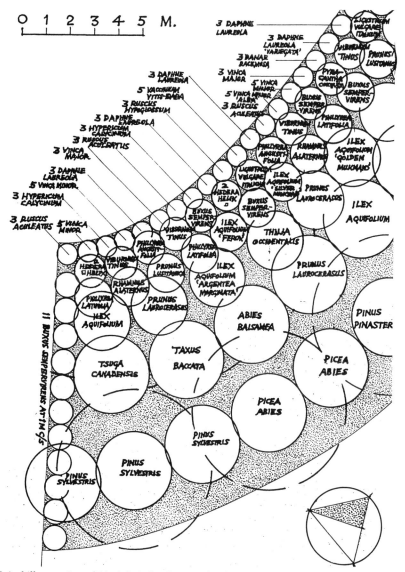

Painshill: a section of Mark Laird's planting plan for the Amphitheatre at Painshill Park, based on a design by Lord Petre (1713-42). (Copyright design: Mark Laird.)

Painshill Park: (left) the Gothic Temple or Pavilion seen from across the lake; (right) a detail of the Pavilion after restoration. (Photographs: John Harvey.)

1773. A great deal of the main planting had been done by 1744, when John Rocque made a detailed survey, and the vineyard or some part of it must have been planted at latest by 1743 to yield the grapes recorded in 1748. Hamilton continued for another quarter century to plant trees, many of them new introductions from America.

The saving of Painshill has involved a large amount of co-operative and largely voluntary effort by individuals and by societies. Among the many to whom particular credit is due must be mentioned the late James Lindus Forge, who with other local enthusiasts formed the Friends of Painshill in 1975. After Elmbridge Borough Council had acquired the land in 1980 the Painshill Park Trust was set up and Mrs Janie Burford appointed director, with Mrs Mavis Collier as archivist and historian. The essential landscape survey was directed by John Phibbs. The Garden History Society and many individual members have provided support throughout, and Michael Symes in particular has researched in detail the archival records of Hamilton's plantings. Further research on the introductions of woody plants has been carried out by Mark Laird, author of the detailed plans for the replanting now actively in progress. Gilbert Williams, as architect, has been responsible for the restoration of the Gothic Temple, or Pavilion, now superbly consolidated and redecorated (see Burford in Conservation 1984).

Another instance of co-operative effort on a grand scale is provided by Mount Edgcumbe, now in Cornwall but formerly a detached part of Devon, a large estate purchased jointly in 1971 by Plymouth City Council and Cornwall County Council and administered as a country park by a joint committee. It is exceptional among the outstanding landscapes of England in having much of its boundaries on the sea coast. Relatively little work has been done as yet on the restoration of the gardens, Italian, French and English, but much clearance has taken place in the landscape and detailed proposals formulated as well as a Management Plan, substantially influenced by the results of very far-reaching researches undertaken by the Garden History Society. There is reason to expect that Mount Edgcumbe will within a few years be one of the most notable garden restorations in the whole of Britain.

Later Georgian gardens

1760-1800

The steady growth of naturalism, already seen in embryo in the 1730s and in the development of the *ferme ornée,* had become fashionable after Kent laid out the Carlton House garden for the Prince of Wales in 1733. In the 1740s came the short interlude of 'rococo' gardening, immortalized in some of the most intriguing views by the painter Thomas Robins the Elder. By 1756 Isaac Ware, in his standard book *A Complete Body of Architecture,* included a warm advocacy of natural planting in his chapters on gardening. Within a few years came the transformation of the Kew Garden of the late Prince of Wales into the principal centre for the introduction of new plants. This was due to the personal interest of the Princess Augusta, widow of the prince and mother of George III. The effective beginning of Kew in its new role can be placed in 1759, when William Aiton was made head gardener, and a year later George III succeeded to the throne. The king was himself interested in gardens as well as in farming, and the new reign was propitious to new developments. Foreign trade, exploration and science went hand in hand, and gardening benefited from the introduction of unknown species more than at any time before or since. It has been calculated that in 1700 some 1,400 foreign kinds had been introduced, and that by 1800 this had increased tenfold to almost 14,000. The first catalogue of the Kew collection, by Sir John Hill, counted 3,389 species in 1768, while the number had risen by 1789 to 5,535 in Aiton's own *Hortus Kewensis.*

Very many of these plants came from hotter regions and could only be grown in hothouses, glasshouses and conservatories, but immense numbers were hardy. Within a single generation the potentialities of the English garden had been revolutionized. To display a large selection of these riches became the ambition of every keen gardener, and this necessarily involved a much less formal style of design. Even the clipped box edgings to beds and borders, almost universal for a hundred years or more, began to give way to mixtures of dwarf flowering plants, often strongly perfumed, such as pinks, violets and mignonette. Trade catalogues provide an infallible index to what was actually being grown on a large scale. Whereas Furber had illustrated 285 sorts of flowering bulbs and herbaceous plants in 1730, the Westminster firm of Webb had 475 in 1760, and in 1771 the great nursery of William Malcolm in Kennington offered 650 sorts as well as 250 flowering trees and shrubs. In another seven years, by 1778, Malcolm had no fewer than 650 different woody plants and 1100 herbaceous and bulbous. There was little room for further expansion, and even Conrad Loddiges of Hackney in 1804 had not many more species.

All this was happening in parallel to the career of Lancelot 'Capability' Brown (1716-83), whose effective work as a designer covered some 35 years from about 1748. Brown has been represented as an opponent of the flower-garden, but this is to misunderstand his role, which was primarily as a designer of wide landscapes. This did not prevent him from using a great variety of trees and flowering shrubs when employed to design a 'wilderness' at Petworth, planted in 1753-57. He got the plants from John Williamson, Furber's successor at the Kensington Nursery. Nearly 40 genera were involved: the main broad-leaved tree was the plane, of which 120 were supplied, with ten evergreen oaks and seven maples, 72 evergreen conifers and 75 larch. Out of 249 flowering trees there were ten arbutus, 30 thorns, 20 laburnum, 58 *Prunus,* 40 *Robinia,* 78 mixed lilacs and ten Guelder Roses. Among the smaller shrubs and climbers were 20 *Hibiscus syriacus,* 30 honeysuckles, 30 *Philadelphus,* 22 sumacs, as well as 270 roses of many varieties.

The summer flowers in a gentleman's garden were recorded by the poet Gray at Stoke Poges in July 1754. Besides fruit, he noted during the month honeysuckles, *Phlomis* or yellow tree-sage, Virginia flowering raspberry, shrub cinque-foil, Spiraea frutex, Syringa (*Philadelphus*), Balm of Gilead (*Cedronella triphylla*), common white and yellow jasmines, white and gum cistus, tamarisk, Coccygria and Virginia sumac, tutsan, Spanish Broom and eleven sorts of roses ending the season, the White Rose the last on 31st July. Gray's garden flowers of July were Convolvulus minor, garden poppy, single and double rose-campion, double larkspur, candytuft, common marigold, pansies, lupins blue, white and yellow (annuals), purple toads-flax, white and blue campanula, double scarlet lychnis, tree primrose (*Oenothera biennis*), white and striped lilies, willow-bay (*Epilobium angustifolium*), scarlet bean (the Scarlet Runner, then still regarded as an ornamental), French marigold, tree-mallow (probably *Lavatera arborea*), amaranthus cats-tail, Fairchild's Mule (the famous hybrid *Dianthus*), African ragwort (*Senecio elegans*), carnations, and double white stock. In 1759 he put down as in bloom on 25th September: red and blue double asters (*Callistephus*), musk and monthly roses, marigolds, sweet peas, carnations, mignonette, double stocks. The general picture was succinctly described by the Scottish writer Tobias Smollett as being the Englishman's expectations of a garden. Writing from the South of France in March 1765 he summed up the English garden as 'clumps of trees, woods and wildernesses cut into delightful alleys perfumed with honeysuckle and with sweet-briar,... (the Englishman) looks for plats of flowers in different parts to refresh the sense, and please the fancy'.

Relatively little is on record concerning the design and planting of town gardens, even those belonging to the nobility and gentry. The plans of a few, of exceptional size, appear on engraved surveys of towns produced in the later part of the eighteenth century, but these are seldom to a sufficiently large scale to show detail or even to provide convincing evidence of reliability. It was correspondingly encouraging that the decision of Bath City Council in 1984 to re-create a period garden behind 4 Circus, a house of 1757-60, should have resulted in the discovery of its actual plan. The wise decision was taken to carry out an archaeological excavation by the Bath Archaeological Trust, whose headquarters share the house with the Bath Museums Service. The investigation under Robert Bell revealed beneath a seal of clay dumped c 1836 a basic platform of compacted gravel between stone-flagged walks flanked by beds inside the walls on each side. At the back, opposite to the house and sheltering the garden from public view, was a large bed containing supports for what was probably a transverse trellised feature of wood. There was no lawn, but in the gravel three beds along the axis, two circular and the central one elliptical. This arrangement echoes the layout of the town plan of this part of Bath by the two architects John Wood, father and son, with the round Circus linked to the semi-elliptical Royal Crescent. A detailed report and plans for restoration have been drawn up by the Garden History Society at the request of Bath City Council. Although too much must not be built upon this single survival of around 1760-90, it shows that even in a fashionable centre the design of gardens might still be formal after the accession of George III.

In the greater gardens of the time there was an uneasy coexistence of the older style, somewhat brightened by the growing cult of flowers, and the new wave of the 'naturalistic' Picturesque seen in its glory at Nuneham Courtenay, Oxford-shire, after 1770 and directly inspired by the Reverend William Mason (1724-97) and his verse treatise *The English Garden*. Nuneham was theoretically based on Julie's garden in the

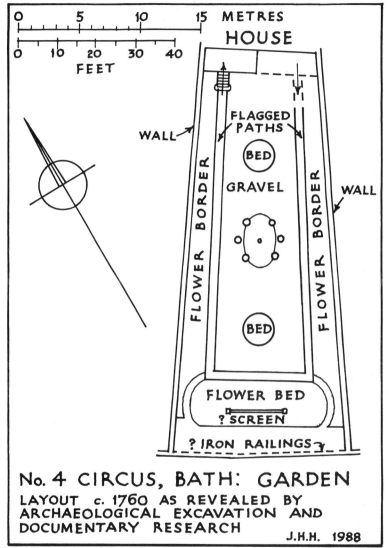

4 Circus, Bath: layout of the garden of 1760 as revealed by excavation in 1985. (Copyright drawing: John Harvey.)

Cadland, Hampshire: (right) part of the landscaping designed by 'Capability' Brown in 1777-80, after clearance in 1982-87; (below) looking from the site of the original cottage into Brown's gravel walk, across the replanted borders. (Photographs: John Harvey.)

Nouvelle Héloîse of Jean Jacques Rousseau, who had stayed with Lord Harcourt at Nuneham in 1766. Enough survived of this part of the grounds for serious restoration to begin in 1982 after detailed research by Mrs Mavis Batey and Richard Bisgrove.

At Cadland, on the Solent in Hampshire, the small landscape of the former Boarn Hill Cottage, designed by Brown in 1777-80, has been in course of restoration by Mrs Maldwin Drummond since 1982, to plans drawn up by Hal Moggridge. Much clearance has been necessary to reveal surviving old trees, including pines and holm oaks, and the perimeter walk relaid with gravel. Close to the modern house which has taken the place of the original *cottage orné*, the old borders have been re-created and the small formal garden ('Tatty's Garden') replanted with dwarf box edging. There is authority for almost all that is being done on Brown's original plan and in other records.

*The Swiss Garden,
Old Warden, Bedford-
shire: (right) the Swiss
Cottage of about 1829,
upper level; (below)
the Tree Shelter.*

1800-1830

The final phase of Georgian gardening was dominated by Humphry Repton although he died in 1818. In spite of Repton's fame in his own time and renewed interest in his style in recent years, it does not seem that any of his Red Books has been used as a direct basis for restoration or re-creation, though some have doubtless been employed as management plans for continued maintenance. Work commonly misattributed to Repton at Ashridge, Hertfordshire, was carried out to a different design by Wyatville and has survived by maintenance rather than by deliberate restoration at any period.

By unexpected ill luck, Repton's scheme for the gardens of the Royal Pavilion, Brighton, Sussex, was rejected, and from 1815 onwards what was done was to the designs of John Nash. The whole area had been changed repeatedly, so that recent restoration has been, perforce, based on scholarly research, under the guidance of the Garden History Society. Work has been in progress since 1983 under the auspices of Brighton Borough Council and the Sussex Historic Gardens Restoration Society.

Another official project is that carried out in 1976-81 by the Bedfordshire County Council on the Swiss Garden at Old Warden. This was designed, certainly after 1825 and perhaps in 1829 or later, as a whim of Robert, 3rd Baron Ongley (1803-77). Although on the very edge of our period, the spirit of the peculiar enterprise was undoubtedly that of the 1820s and may be directly due to the employment of the architect Peter Frederick Robinson (1776-1858) who had visited Switzerland between 1816 and 1819 and designed the famous Swiss Cottage in London, built in 1829-32. The Swiss Garden at Old Warden had come into existence by 1832 and the cast ironwork of its greenhouse was made between 1830 and 1833 at the Eagle Foundry, Northampton. The original layout appears on the Ordnance Survey plan made in 1834 and published in the following year. In 1872 Lord Ongley sold the estate to the Shuttleworth family and a 'restoration', largely a Victorianisation, was in progress in 1876-7. After a lengthy period of dereliction the County Council secured a long lease of the property in 1976 and a thorough restoration of the garden and its features has been in progress since.

The Swiss Garden, Old Warden: (above) the transept of the Grotto with cast ironwork of 1830-33; (below left) the Kiosk seen from the bridge; (below right) the Grotto, looking towards the transept.

Epilogue

As we have seen, serious attempts to restore gardens to their appearance at a given date and with authentic planting, have been attempted only in recent years. The total number of such restorations and re-creations dealt with in this book amounts to fewer than thirty, and of these only twenty are regularly open to the public. Many comparable projects are in contemplation or in progress but it may be some years before they can be complete. In cases where substantial work towards such a project has already been done, it seems worthwhile to give outline particulars, here arranged in historical order.

At Basing House in Hampshire, the site of the famous Civil War siege of 1643-45, archaeological excavations have taken place in the area of the Walled Garden after much historical research on the gardens, which were begun soon after 1530. Of later sixteenth-century date was the garden behind the Elizabethan House in the Plymouth Barbican, 32 New Street. It is hoped there to undertake reconstruction of a typical town garden of the period on the steep narrow plot which runs uphill behind the house.

The National Trust is, by stages, restoring the old gardens at Belton House, Lincolnshire, of c 1700, and at Canons Ashby, Northamptonshire, where a formal garden was made in 1710. Under an independent trust extensive research has been done on the contemporary gardens of Castle Bromwich Hall, Warwickshire (West Midlands) and a full survey has been carried out under John Phibbs. Intensive projects for garden restoration, involving tree surveys, archaeology, and research on planting, have been in progress for some years at Mount Edgcumbe, Cornwall, as already mentioned (page 59); and at Chiswick House, Middlesex (London), for the London Borough of Hounslow. In both cases the original gardens were made in successive stages throughout the period from 1725 to 1800, giving rise to complex problems for the restorers. Rather later in the eighteenth century are the ornamental walks of Hawkstone Park, Shropshire, where a survey has been made, and work is in progress for Portsmouth City Council towards a major restoration of the gardens at Leigh Park, Hampshire, the home of the Stauntons who were influential in the introduction of plants from China from 1794 until the death of Sir George Thomas Staunton in 1859.

The recent metamorphosis of the Ancient Monuments Branch

of the old Office of Works into the independent Historic Buildings and Monuments Commission (English Heritage) and the continued acquisition of major properties by the National Trust are already having important consequences for archaeology and for display, and it is likely that they will lead also to further examples of restoration and re-creation of period gardens.

Bibliography and abbreviations

Anthony 1985: Anthony, John. *Discovering Period Gardens.* Shire Publications, first edition 1972.

Aram (1725): Aram, Peter. *A Practical Treatise of Flowers* (edited by F. Felsenstein). Leeds Philosophical and Literary Society, 1985.

Conservation 1984: *The Conservation of Historic Gardens.* Proceedings of a Symposium held by the Garden History Society and the Ancient Monuments Society, 9th May 1984. Introduction by Lord Montagu of Beaulieu and contributions by Mrs Mavis Batey, Mrs Janie Burford, Merrick Denton-Thompson, Duncan Donald, Paul Edwards, Peter Goodchild, John Harvey, Dame Jennifer Jenkins, Dr Sylvia Landsberg, John Sales, Matthew Saunders.

Desmond 1977: Desmond, Ray. *Dictionary of British and Irish Botanists and Horticulturists.* Taylor and Francis.

— 1984: *Bibliography of British Gardens.* St Paul's Bibliographies.

Gerard 1633: Gerard, John. *The Herball* (1597) (revised and enlarged by Thomas Johnson). Facsimile, Dover Publications, New York.

GH: *Garden History.* The Journal of the Garden History Society, annually from 1972.

Halliwell 1987: Halliwell, Brian. *Old Garden Flowers.* Bishopsgate Press.

Hanmer 1659: *The Garden Book of Sir Thomas Hanmer, Bart.* (edited by I. Elstob). Gerald Howe, 1933.

Harvey 1972: Harvey, John. *Early Gardening Catalogues.* Phillimore.

— 1974: *Early Nurserymen.* Phillimore.

— 1981: *Mediaeval Gardens.* Batsford.

Hume 1974: Hume, Audrey N. *Archaeology and the Colonial Gardener.* Colonial Williamsburg Foundation.

Jacques 1978: Jacques, David. 'Restoring Historic Gardens and Parks', *Journal of the Historic Houses Association.*

— 1983: *Georgian Gardens: the Reign of Nature.* Batsford.

Lawson 1617: Lawson, William. *The Country House-Wife's Garden* (edited by Rosemary Verey). Breslich and Foss, 1983.

— 1618: *A New Orchard & Garden* (edited by Eleanour S. Rohde). Cresset Press 1927.

Leith-Ross 1984: Leith-Ross, Prudence. *The John Tradescants.* Peter Owen.

Miller 1754: Miller, Philip. *The Gardeners Dictionary.* Abridged edition 1754 (edited by W. T. Stearn). J. Cramer and Wheldon and Wesley, 1969.

NT: National Trust.

NTS: National Trust for Scotland.

Oxford 1986: Goode, Patrick and Lancaster, Michael, editors. *The Oxford Companion to Gardens.* Oxford University Press.

Parkinson 1629: Parkinson, John. *A Garden of Pleasant Flowers. (Paradisus Terrestris).* Facsimile, Dover Publications, New York.

Sanecki 1987: Sanecki, Kay N. *Discovering Gardens in Britain.* Shire Publications, first edition 1979.

Strong 1979: Strong, Roy. *The Renaissance Garden in England.* Thames and Hudson.

Taylor 1983: Taylor, Christopher. *The Archaeology of Gardens.* Shire Publications.

Taylor and Hill 1983: Taylor, M., and Hill, C. *Hardy Plants introduced to Britain by 1799.* Second edition revised, Cranborne Plant Centre.

Thomas 1984: Thomas, Graham Stuart. *Recreating the Period Garden.* Collins, for the National Trust. Contributions by Paul Edwards, Brent Elliott, Lady O'Neill, Anthony du Gard Pasley, Kay Sanecki, Fred Whitsey.

Appendix 1: Plant lists by periods

Particular thanks are due to Richard Gorer for much help in identifications. For Roses see Appendix 2. See Halliwell 1987 for much useful information.

SUMMARY OF SOURCES

Middle ages 1066-1485

Generally, see identified and dated list of over 250 plants in Harvey 1981, 163-80. Some corrections should be made:

page 169, Buckthorn: delete entry and transfer all occurrences to Gooseberry, page 172.

page 171, Dittany: it is probable that all the British occurrences, X X X, refer to Dittander, above.

page 172, Gentian: delete the British occurrences which refer to Baldmoney (*Meum athamanticum* Jacq.).

c 1300: identified list of 100 plants grown by Henry the Poet (J. Harvey in GH, XV, 1 [1987] 1-11).

c 1340: identified list of 100 plants grown by Master John Gardener (J. Harvey in GH, XIII, 2 [1985] 83-101).

See also Harvey 1974, Appendix II, 138-44, to which the following corrections should be made:

page 142: for 'CARSYNDYLLYS' read as two entries:

CRESSES, ? *Rorippa nasturcium-aquaticum*

DILL, *Peucedanum graveolens*

for Dittany read DITTANDER, *Lepidium latifolium*.

Tudor 1485-1540

See Harvey 1981, 163-80 (to AD 1538).

c 1525 - 40: the 'Fromond' list, in Harvey 1972, 58-64, to which the following corrections should be made:

page 62, Longdebeff: identify as *Picris echioides*.

page 63, Palma Christi: delete queried identification as *Orchis maculata*.

Selian — insert possible identification as ? *Centaurea cyanus*.

Tudor 1540-1603

1548: William Turner, *The Names of Herbes* (with identifications by W. T. Stearn). The Ray Society, 1965.

1596-99: *Plants cultivated in the Garden of John Gerard*, edited with identifications by B. D. Jackson, London, 1876.

Stuart 1603-1660
In general, see Parkinson 1629; Gerard 1633; Hanmer 1659.
   1617 See Lawson 1617. Lawson's plants are here identified and listed alphabetically under their Latin binomials (see below, page 76). See also Lawson 1618.
   1629-34: Tradescant's lists, identified in Leith-Ross 1984, 199-203, 207-21.
   1639: List of seeds sown in April (see below, page 77).
   1656: Tradescant's list, identified in Leith-Ross 1984, 252-92.

Stuart 1660-1714
   1677: list of William Lucas, identified in Harvey 1972, 66-74, to which these corrections should be made:
page 68, Potherbs, Langdebeefe: identify as *Picris echioides*.
page 69, Flowers, White Wallflower: identify as *Matthiola incana* var. *graeca*.
   London Pride: identify as *Dianthus barbatus*.
page 70, Fox Tail: identify as ? *Lagurus ovatus*.
   1684: Roger Looker's bill for Longleat, identified in GH, XI, 1 (1983) 30-1.
   1688: George Rickets' catalogue, identified in Harvey 1974, 146-9, to which the following corrections should be made:
page 146, 'Pardus' Theophrasti should read 'Padus' and be identified as *Prunus fruticosa (chamaecerasus)*.
page 147, Virginian Climer: identify as *Parthenocissus quinquefolia*.
   Upright Savin: identify as *Juniperus thurifera*.
page 149, Gentianella: delete query and 'or G. Verna'.

Early Georgian 1714-1760
See Aram (1725); Miller 1754.
   1724, 1727, 1730: the catalogues of Robert Furber of Kensington, identified (see below, page 78).

Late Georgian 1760-1800
   1775: A Catalogue of Forest Trees, Fruit Trees, Ever-Green and Flowering-Shrubs sold by John & George Telford, York. Facsimile identified in Harvey 1972, 83-99.
   1782: A Catalogue of Hardy Trees, Shrubs, ... Herbaceous Plants sold by John Kingston Galpine, Blandford. Facsimile with commentary including identifications in *The Georgian Garden*, Dovecote Press, 1983.
   1778-85: for the plants and seeds available from leading

nurserymen, identified lists are held by the Garden History Society, covering woody plants, herbaceous, annuals, biennials and bulbs. The Society intends to publish these lists.

Late Georgian 1800-1830

1829: Loudon, J. C. *Encyclopaedia of Plants.* The original edition (later reprinted with supplements) includes all plants native or introduced, with numerous woodcuts. Dates of introductions are given among much other information on every plant.

1833: Mackie, F., Norwich. Prices of Trees and Shrubs. Facsimile in Harvey 1972, 142-51.

1835, 1837: A Catalogue of Seeds ... / ... Flower - Roots, sold by Flanagan and Nutting, London. Facsimiles in Harvey 1972, 120-41.

Reference should be made to M. Taylor and C. Hill, *Hardy Plants introduced to Britain by 1799,* second revised and enlarged edition 1983, Cranborne Garden Centre, Dorset. It should be noted that this excludes annuals and also most plants native to Britain. All other plants are listed sectionally: Bulbs, Tubers and Corms; Hardy Perennial Plants; Ornamental Shrubs; Climbers; Trees; Conifers; with dates of introduction.

In view of the repeated alterations in strictly botanical nomenclature the Latin binomials used here are, as far as possible, in accordance with the *Dictionary of Gardening* of the Royal Horticultural Society, second edition 1956, corrected 1965. Other names in current use are added in brackets, with cross-references in the cases of change of genus.

PLANT LISTS

1617: William Lawson's plants from *The Country House-Wife's Garden,* identified and arranged alphabetically by Latin binomials. Lawson's division into Tall, Medium and Dwarf plants is here marked by indenting, tall to the left.

Alcea (Althaea) rosea Hollihock
  Allium cepa Onions
  Allium fistulosum Chibbals
  Allium porrum Leeks
  Allium sativum Garlick
  Allium schoenoprasum Chives
 Anchusa officinalis Bugloss
Angelica archangelica Angelica
 Anthemis nobilis Camomile
 Anthriscus cerefolium Charvel
Artemisia abrotanum Southernwood
  Bellis perennis Daisies
 Borago officinalis Burrage
 Brassica oleracea Cabbages
  Brassica rapa Turnip
 Calendula officinalis Mary-golds, Marigolds
  Centaurium erythraea Centaury
  Cheiranthus cheiri Wall-flowers, Bee-flowers
   Chrysanthemum balsamita Coast
 Chrysanthemum parthenium Feather-few
Chrysanthemum (Tanacetum) vulgare Tansie
Cichorium endivia Endive
Cichorium intybus Succory
  Cnicus benedictus Carduus-Benedictus, or Blessed Thistle
 Coriandrum sativum Coriander
Crataegus oxyacantha Thorn
  Crocus sativus Saffron
 Cucurbita pepo Pumpions
Cynara scolymus Artichoaks
  Daucus carota Carrets
  Dianthus spp. Pinks
 Dianthus caryophyllus July-flowers, Gilly-flowers
Foeniculum vulgare Fennel
  Fragaria vesca Strawberries
 Glycyrrhiza glabra Licoras
 Hyssopus officinalis Isop, Hysop
Inula helenium Elicampane
 Iris florentina Flower-de-luce
 Iris germanica Flower-de-luce
  Lactuca sativa Lettice
 Lavandula spica Lavender-spike
 Lavandula spica alba White Lavender
Levisticum officinale Lovage
Ligustrum vulgare Privit
Lilium bulbiferum Red Lilly
Lilium candidum White Lilly

Malva crispa French Mallows, Gagged Mallows
Matthiola incana Stock-Gilliflowers
Mentha spp. Garden-Mints
  Mentha pulegium Penny-royal or Pudding-grass
Myrrhis odorata Sweet Sicily
  Narcissus pseudonarcissus Daffadowndillies
  Origanum majorana Marjoram
Paeonia spp. Piony
Papaver somniferum French Poppy
  Pastinaca sativa Parsnips
  Petroselinum crispum Parsly
  Picris echioides Langdibeef
  Pimpinella anisum Aniseeds
  Primula veris Cowslips
  Ranunculus aconitifolius flore pleno Bachelors buttons
  Raphanus sativus Raddish
Ribes nigrum Raisins
Ribes uva-crispa Fea-berries
Rosa spp. Roses
Rosmarinus officinalis Rosemary
Ruta graveolens Rue, or Herb of Grace
Salvia sclarea Clary
  Salvia officinalis Sage
  Salvia verbenaca Oculus Christi or Christ's-eye
  Satureia hortensis Savory
  Sium sisarum Skerots
  Smyrnium olusatrum Alexanders
  Teucrium chamaedrys Germander
  Thymus vulgaris Time
  Tragopogon pratensis Go to bed at noon
Valeriana officinalis Valerian
  Viola odorata Violets
  Viola tricolor Pansie, or Heartsease

1639: Seeds sown on 6th April (from Sloane MS 95, f. 153). For a discussion of this list see Harvey 1972, 13.

Adonis annua Rose Rubie
Antirrhinum majus Snapdragons of divers collours
Aquilegia vulgaris Dubble Collumbines, Red, white & blewe
?Aristolochia serpentaria Serpentarius
Datura stramonium Thorne Apple
Dianthus caryophyllus Doubble gilliflowers
Hedysarum coronarium French honisuckles
Iberis umbellata Tuft of Candie
Impatiens balsamina Balsum foemina
Lathyrus latifolius Pease flower
Lunaria biennis Honesti
Lupinus hirsutus, L. varius Lupins blew
Lupinus luteus Lupins yellow
Lupinus sp. Spanish lupins
  (*L. angustifolius*, from Spain, is said not to have been introduced until 1686)

Matthiola incana Stockes purple & white
?Nigella damascena Nigella Romana
Oenothera biennis Primrose flower
Paeonia mascula, P. officinalis Pionii
Primula auricula Auriculaes
Ricinus communis Palma Christi
Saxifraga umbrosa (x urbium) Prince's feather
Scilla amoena Turkie starre
Scorzonera hispanica Viper flower
Tagetes erecta The greate African marigold
Tagetes patula The knotted marigold
Tragopogon porrifolius (Purple) ⎫ Go to bed at noone
Tragopogon pratensis (Yellow) ⎭
Tulipa gesneriana Tulips

1724-1730: Robert Furber's catalogues, Kensington. Three catalogues of Furber's nursery survive: that printed by Philip Miller in 1724 as an appendix to *The Gardener's and Florist's Dictionary,* volume II, with Latin names for most of the woody species; Furber's own catalogue of trees, shrubs and climbers dated 1727 (of which copies survive, with his catalogue of fruit-trees, in the Bodleian Library at Oxford and in the British Library); and the list to be deduced from the frontispiece and twelve plates of his *Twelve Months of Flowers* issued in 1730-32. It is only from this collection of engravings that the names of the principal annuals and biennials can be derived.

Almost all of Furber's plants can be identified with certainty or with a high degree of probability (the latter marked here with ?). In a few instances there is serious doubt (marked with??), and two plants, though depicted in 1730, have so far eluded identification altogether: 'Virginia [sic] Shrub Acre' (number 31 in October), and 'Sage & Rosemary Tree' (number 26 in December). All the rest are here arranged in three series: Trees and Shrubs; Herbaceous Perennials and Bulbs; Annuals and Biennials. Tender plants are marked T, but hardiness is relative and this may indicate anything from a stove plant to one moderately hardy in favoured areas.

Plants prefixed with 1727 or 1730 are first found in those lists respectively; all others are based on the entries of 1724, adding the Latin name only in cases of doubt as to identity. Additional English names from the two later lists are given only where they differ significantly or add to the evidence for identification.

The Catalogue of Robert Furber of Kensington, 1724-1730
Trees and shrubs

Abies alba		Firr, called Silver Firr	c 1603
Abies balsamea		Balm of Gilead Firr	1697
Acacia farnesiana	1730	Acacia, or sweet button tree (T)	1656
Acer campestre		Common Wood Maple Tree, or the lesser English sort	——
Acer negundo		Ash leav'd Maple of Virginia	1688
Acer platanoides		Norway Maple with a plane-Tree leaf	(1683)
(variegatum)	1727	ditto with stripe'd Leaves	
Acer pseudoplatanus		Great Maple, falsely called the Sycamore	c 1550
albovariegatum		ditto with strip'd Leaves	

Acer rubrum		Virginian flowering Maple	c 1650
Acer saccharinum	1730	American flowering Maple	1725
Adhatoda vasica		Malabar Nut (T)	1699
Aesculus hippocastanum		Horse Chesnut Tree	c 1616
variegatum	1727	ditto with strip'd Leaves	
Aesculus pavia		Horse Chesnut Tree with scarlet Flowers	1711
Alnus glutinosa		Alder-tree	—
	1727	the English narrow-leav'd	
	1727	the Dutch broad-leav'd	
Aloe spp.		Aloes twelve sorts (T)	

(Identification in any precise sense is impossible, but four sorts are named in 1730: Grey Aloe (? *A. glauca*); Spotted Aloe (? *A. variegata*); Yellow Dwarf Aloe (? *A. humilis*); Scarlet African Aloe with Pineapple Leaves (*A. arborescens*). Other species likely to have been stocked are *A. barbadiensis* (*vera*); *A. saponaria*; and *A. succotrina*. It is not improbable that several kinds of Agave were included as 'aloes', notably *Agave americana, A. lurida,* and *A. vivipara*.)

Ampelopsis arborea		Parsley leav'd Virginian Climber called the Pepper Tree	1700
Anagyris foetida	1727	Bean-Trefoile, a large Tree (T)	1570
Anthyllis barba-jovis	1727	Barba Jovis, or Silver-bush (T)	1640
Aralia spinosa	1727	Angelica Spinosa, a Tree of Carolina	1688
Arbutus unedo		Arbutus, or Strawberry Tree	—
	1727	the Irish sort	
	1727	from Genoua	
	1730	Arbutus double	
Aronia arbutifolia		Dwarf Mespilus, or Bastard Quince *Mespilus folio sub-rotundo, fructu rubro*	1700
	1727	Medlar, the Dwarf, flowering, of Virginia	
Aronia melanocarpa	1727	Mespilus of Virginia, with black Fruit	c 1700
Artemisia absinthium	1727	Wormwood-Tree	—
Athanasia trifurcata	1730	Trifid African Golden Knob (T)	1710
Atriplex halimus		Halimus, Sea Purslain, or Orach Tree	1632
Baccharis halimifolia		Groundsel Tree from Virginia	1683 ·
Berberis canadensis		Canada Berberry	'1759'
	1727	Barberry-Tree, from Canada	
Berberis vulgaris		Berberry	—
asperma		ditto without Stones	
alba		ditto with white Fruit	
Betula pubescens		Birch-Tree	—
	1727	the English sort	

(Note: *Betula pendula* was considered a new sort, not on the market until c 1785; see *Quarterly Journal of Forestry*, LXVII, 1973, 25)

Bupleurum fruticosum		Sisseli *Sesseli Aethiopicum frutex*	
	1727	Seseli Ethiopicum, Hart-wort	1596
Buxus sempervirens		Box-Tree	—

aureomarginata		ditto with strip'd Leaves	
suffruticosa		Dwarf Dutch Box	

(1727 has the English sort, for Standards; the Dutch, for Standards; the Dutch, finely variegated; the shining Olive-leav'd; the Dutch Dwarf, for Edgings)

?*Caesalpinia (Poinciana)*	1727	Bean-Trefoile,	
pulcherrima		from Barbadoes (T)	*1690*
		Laburnum, from Barbadoes	
Campsis radicans		Trumpet Flower	1640
	1727	Trumpet Flower, the Major	
Campsis radicans minor		Trumpet Flower of Virginia with Orange coloured Leaves	1640
	1727	Trumpet Flower, the Minor, of Virginia	
Capparis spinosa		Caper Bush; True Caper (T)	1596
Carpinus betulus		Horn-beam Tree	——
variegata	1727	ditto, the English, stripe'd	
Carya ovata		Hickery Walnut from Carolina	1629
Castanea pumila		Chinquapin, or dwarf Virginian Chesnut	1699
Castanea sativa		Common, or Spanish Chesnut-Tree	
variegata		ditto, with striped Leaves	
?? *Ceanothus americanus*	1727	Pecia, ever green like a Phillyrea	1713
Cedrus libani		Cedar of Lebanon	c 1638
? *Celtis australis*		Lotus, or Nettle Tree	1596
Cercis siliquastrum		Judas Tree	1596
	1727	Arbor Judae, with single flowers	
	1727	ditto, with double flowers	
	1727	Arbor Judae, the Tree of Love from Spain	
Chamaecyparis — see *Juniperus virginiana caroliniana*			
Chionanthus virginicus		Snow-drop Tree *Frutex viola bulbosa data* (? *dicta*)	'1736'

(Note: *Halesia* was not called Snowdrop Tree until after 1780)

Chrysanthemum frutescens		Canary Pellitory (T)	1699
Cistus sp.		Cistus, or Holy Rose	
? *C. albidus*	1727	ditto, long-leave'd	1596
? *C. salvifolius*	1727	ditto, round-leave'd	1548
Citrus aurantiifolia		Lime (T)	1648
Citrus aurantium		Sevil Orange (and varieties) (T)	1595
	1730	ditto, Striped	
Citrus limonia (limon)		Common Lemon (and varieties) (T)	1648
	1730	Lisbon Lemmon-Tree (T)	
Citrus maxima		Pumpelmoes or Shaddock (T)	1722
Citrus medica		Citron (T)	1648

Citrus sinensis		China Orange (and varieties) (T)	1595
Clematis cirrhosa		Spanish Virgin's Bower	1596
	1727	the single Spanish White	
Clematis crispa		Flowering Climber from Mr. Dubois's at Mitcham, a Sort of Virgin's Bower	'1726'
	1727	Clematis of Virginia, Willow-leaved; Bower, the single Willow-leav'd	
Clematis viticella		Virgin's Bower with single Flowers	1569
plena		ditto with double Flowers	
	1727	Virgin's Bower, the double Purple	
Colutea arborescens	1727	Bladder Sena, a Flowering Shrub; the Bladder Sena, large	1548
Colutea orientalis	1730	Red Oriental Colutea	1710
Coriaria myrtifolia		Myrtle leav'd Sumach	1629
Cornus amomum	1727	Dogwood, the Virginia sort	1683
Cornus mas		Cornelian Cherry Tree	? c 1350
Cornus sanguinea		Dogwood Tree; the English sort	——
variegata	1727	ditto with striped Leaves	
Coronilla argentea		Coronilla with silver Leaves, or yellow Collutea; Silver leav'd Coronilla (T)	1664
Coronilla emerus	1727	Sena the Scorpion, a Shrub	1596
? *Corylus rostrata (cornuta)*	1727	Nut of America, bearing in Tufts	'1745'
Corylus maxima	1727	Filberd; the Spanish, or Cob Filberd, Filbert Tree	
Cotinus — see *Rhus*			
Crataegus azarolus		Azeroli from Naples	1629
Crataegus coccinea (pedicellata)	1727	Mespilus of Virginia, with red Fruit	1683
Crataegus crus-galli		Mespilus, or large Cock Spur thorn; Hawthorn, with Cock-spur Thorns	1691
Crataegus monogyna praecox (biflora)		Glastenbury, or Christmas Thorn	——
Crataegus oxyacantha		Mespilus, or common Hawthorn	——
plena		ditto, with double Flowers	
? *fructu luteo*	1727	Hawthorn, the English, with white Fruit	
Crataegus uniflora		Azeroli with Pyracantha leaves *Mespilus spinosa pyri folio*	1704
Cupressus sempervirens		Common Cypress, or upright (T) c 1375	
Cupressus horizontalis		Male Cypress, or spreading Cypress (T)	
	1727	ditto, the Italian, great sort (T)	
? *Cydonia oblonga*		Quince from New England *Malus cotonea Americana*	

(Probably a quince taken out by the early settlers and mistakenly thought to be American)

Latin name		English name	
Cytisus sessilifolius		Cytisus secundus Clusii	1629
Danaë racemosa		Alexandrian Laurel	1713
Daphne laureola	1727	Spurge-Laurel, the plain sort	——
(variegata)	1727	ditto with stripe'd Leaves	
Daphne mezereum		Mezereon	c 1561
	1727	with deep-red Flowers	
	1727	with Peach coloured Flowers	
alba	1727	with white Flowers	
(variegata)	1727	with strip'd Leaves	
Diospyros virginiana		Pishamin of Virginia	1629
Dorycnium rectum	1727	Dorychnium, a Flowering Shrub	1640
? Doxantha capreolata	1727	Creeper, the Virginia Flowering	1710
Elaeagnus angustifolia		Oleaster, or wild Olive	c 1550
Euonymus europaeus	1727	Eunonymus, or Spindle-Tree, the English	——
Euonymus latifolius	1727	Eunonymus, the Hungarian, broad-leave'd	'1730'
Fagus sylvatica		Beech-Tree; the common English	——
Ficus sycomorus	1727	Fig-tree, with Zacheus his Sycamore-fruit; Sycamore Fig (T)	(1727)
Fraxinus americana	1727	Ash from Carolina, with white Keys	1724
Fraxinus excelsior		Ash-Tree; the common English	——
argenteo-variegata		ditto, with strip'd Leaves	1700
Fraxinus ornus	1727	Ash, the Italian, with white Flowers	
Fraxinus parvifolia		Manna-Ash	1697
(rotundifolia)	1727	Ash, the Dew, or the Manna-Ash	
Gelsemium sempervirens		Jassemine of Virginia with yellow Flowers; broad-leaved (T)	1640
Genista (Lygos) monosperma	1727	Spanish Broom, with white Flowers	1690
Genista tinctoria	1727	Genista, a small Flowering Shrub	——
Gleditschia (Gleditsia) triacanthos		Acacia or Honey Locust of Virginia; treble thorn'd	c 1690
Gossypium arboreum	1730	Shrub Cotton (T)	1694
Hedera helix		Ivy Tree	——
arborescens	1727	Ivy, the broad-leave'd Tree, kind for Heads	
	1727	ditto, the small creeping kind, stripe'd	
		Ivy with striped Leaves	

Hibiscus syriacus		Althea Frutex	1596
	1727	ditto, with white Bloom	
	1727	ditto, with red Bloom	
	1727	ditto, with purple Bloom	
	1727	ditto, with striped Leaves	
Hippophaë rhamnoides		Buckthorn with Willow Leaves; Sea-Buckthorn	——
Hypericum balearicum	1730	Myrto-Cistus (T)	1714
Hypericum canariense	1727	Hypericum, a Shrub from the Canaries (T)	1699
Hypericum hircinum	1727	St. John's-Wort, a yellow flowering Shrub	1640
Iberis semperflorens	1730	Tree Candy Tuft (T)	1679
Ilex aquifolium		Holly Tree	——

(varieties: with yellow Berries; 1727 ditto stripe'd; 1727 with white Berries; Hedg-hog Holly, plain; Blind's Cream; Fine Phyllis, yellow; Fine Union, best yellow; Bagshot's Yellow; Gold Edger; Bridgman's, white; Broderick's white; Partridge's, yellow; Milkmaid; Eales's, white; Painted Lady, white; Hertfordshire White; Silver-edg'd Hedg-hog; Gold edg'd Hedg-hog; Gold bloatch'd Hedg-hog; 1727 the Pritchet's, yellow)

Ilex vomitoria (cassine)		Cassine, or South-Sea Tea Tree (T)	1700
	1727	Cassine, with dented Leaves	
angustifolia		ditto, with long smooth Leaves (T)	
	1727	? Holly, the narrow-leave'd of Carolina	
Isoplexis canariensis	1730	Canary shrub foxglove (T)	1698
Jasminum azoricum		Ivy leav'd white Jassemine (T)	c 1719
Jasminum grandiflorum		Catalonian or Spanish Jassemine (T)	1629
	1730	Spanish white Jasmine	
Jasminum grandiflorum floribus plenis	1730	Double Spanish Jasmine (T)	1629
Jasminum humile		Jassemine with yellow Flowers	1634
Jasminum odoratissimum	1730	Indian yellow Jasmine (T)	1656
Jasminum officinale		Jassemine with white Flowers a common Jassemine	c 1500
foliis argenteis	1727	with silver-edged Leaves	
aureovariegatum	1727	with bloached Leaves	
Jasminum sambac flore pleno		Arabian Jassemine (T)	1665
	1730	Double Arabian Jasmine	
? *Juglans cinerea* form		Dwarf Walnut from Carolina	1633
		Nux juglans pumila Caroliniana	
	1727	Walnut, the Dwarf, of Carolina	
Juglans nigra		Black Walnut from Virginia	1629
Juglans regia		Walnut Tree	c 1200
		Great French Walnut	
Juniperus bermudiana		Cedar of Bermudas (T)	1683
Juniperus communis		Common Juniper	——

Latin name		Common name	
		Standards	
suecica		Swedish Juniper	1701
	1727	Juniper, the Sweedish, for close Trees	
Juniperus sabina		Savin Tree	c 1200
Juniperus virginiana		Cedar of Virginia	c 1664
caroliniana	1727	Cedar, the White, from Carolina	'1736'
? or Chamaecyparis thyoides			
Laburnum anagyroides		Laburnum	1560
Lantana camara		Viburnum Americanum; American Viburnum (T)	1691
Larix decidua		Larix, or Larch Tree	c 1620
	1727	ditto, grows high	
	1730	White-flowering Larch tree	
? Larix laricina	1730	Red-flowering Larch-tree	'1739'
Laurus nobilis		Bay-Tree	
angustifolia		ditto with narrow Leaves	
		Dutch Bay, smooth shining-leav'd	
variegata		Bay with strip'd Leaves	
	1727	Bay, the English, bloach'd with Yellow	
	1727	ditto, tipt with White	
Lavandula dentata	1730	Lavender with divided Leaves (T)	1597
Leonotis leonurus		Leonorusses two Sorts (1); Archangel Tree (T)	1712
Leonotis ovata		Leonorusses two Sorts (2) (T)	1713
Ligustrum vulgare		Privet, or Prick Timber	——
variegatum	1727	ditto, with yellow bloached Leaves	
	1727	ditto, with white bloached Leaves	
sempervirens		Privet, Italian Ever-green	?
Lindera benzoin		Benjamin Tree; from Carolina	1683
Liquidambar styraciflua		Maple leaved Storax; Storax-Tree, liquid Amber	1681
Liriodendron tulipifera		Tulip Tree with Maple Leaves	1638
Lonicera alpigena		Red berried, upright Honey-Suckle	1596
Lonicera x americana	1730	Ever green Honeysuckle	(1716)
Lonicera caprifolium		Italian Honey-Suckle	?
		Early flowering Honey-Suckle	
Lonicera coerulea		Blue berried, upright Honey-Suckle	1629
Lonicera periclymenum belgica		Dutch Honey-Suckle	——
Lonicera periclymenum serotina	1730	Long blowing Honeysuckle	——
Lonicera sempervirens		Honey Suckles with the Leaves always green	1656
	1727	Honeysuckle, the Virginia,	

		scarlet Posthorn; the Ever-green, Winter flowering	
Lonicera xylosteum		Fly Honey-Suckle	—
Lygos — see *Genista*			
Malus coronaria		Crab tree of Virginia with sweet Flowers	1717
Malus pumila (domestica)			
? *astrachanica*		Apple-Tree from Muscovy (Probably 'White Astrakhan' = 'Muscovite Transparent' 1653)	
	1727	Apple-Tree with bloached Leaves	
	1727	Apple without Blossom	
	1727	Crab-Tree, with stripe'd Leaves	
Medicago arborea		Cytisus lunatus; Moon Trefoile (T)	1596
Menispermum canadense		Convolvulus Tree, a Species of Ivy from Virginia, according to Dr Pluknet	? 1634
Mespilus germanica		Common Medlar	
		Great manured Medlar	
	1727	the common English sort	
	1727	the great Dutch sort	
Morus alba		Mulberry Tree with white Fruit	1596
	1727	Mulberry from France, with white Fruit	
Morus nigra		Mulberry Tree with black Fruit	?
	1727	ditto, the black, with stripe'd Leaves	
Morus rubra	1727	Mulberry of Carolina, with large Leaves	1629
Myrica cerifera		Candle-Berry Tree from Virginia	1699
	1727	ditto, with Olive-Leaves	
? *latifolia*	1727	ditto, with Hawthorn Leaves, ever green	1699
Myrica gale		Sweet Gaule, Sweet Willow, or Dutch Myrtle	—
Myricaria germanica		Shrub Tamarisk, or German Tamarisk	1582
Myrtus communis		Myrtle	1597
flore pleno		Double flowering Myrtle	1597
baetica		Orange leav'd Myrtle	
buxifolia		Box leav'd Myrtle	
argenteo-variegata		ditto, strip'd	
erecta		Upright Myrtle	
argenteo-variegata		ditto, strip'd	
lusitanica		Broad leav'd Portugal Myrtle	
microphylla		Thyme leav'd Myrtle	
moscata		Nutmeg Myrtle	
argenteo-striata		ditto, Strip'd	

rosmarinifolia		Rosemary leav'd Myrtle	
		Birds-nest Myrtle	
Nerium oleander	1730	Red Oleander (T)	1596
album	1730	White Oleander (T)	
Oftia (Spielmannia) africana		Ilex leav'd Jassemine (T)	1710
Olea europaea		Olive with broad Leaves, or	
		Manured, or Garden Olive	
		Tree (T)	1570
	1727	Olive from Italy, with broad	
		Leaves	
		Luca Olive	
	1727	the Luke-Olive from Spain	
		Olive with Box Leaves	
	1727	Olive, the small round-leaved,	
		like Box-Leaves	
	1727	Olive from Genoua, with broad	
		Leaves	
Ostrya carpinifolia		Hop Horn-beam Tree	1724
Ostrya virginiana	1727	Hornbeam of Virginia, with	
		long Leaves; Hornbeam, the	
		flowering of Virginia	1692
? *var.*		Horn-beam from Virginia with	
		small Leaves like the small	
		leav'd Elm	
? *Oxydendrum arboreum*	1727	Spinage-Tree	'1752'
Paliurus spina-Christi	1727	Christ's Thorn	1596
Parthenocissus quinquefolia	1727	Creeper, the Indian climbing	
		sort	1629
Passiflora caerulea		The common broad leav'd	
		Passion Flower (T)	1699
var.		The narrow leav'd, or Fruit	
		bearing Passion Flower	
		Grenadilla pentaphyllos, flore	
		caeruleo magno (T)	
Passiflora lutea		The yellow Passion Flower (T)	1714
? *Persea borbonia pubescens*	1727	Bay from Carolina, the narrow-	
		leav'd (T)	'1739'
Persea indica	1727	Roman or Laurus Regia;	
		Victoria's Laurij (T)	1665
Philadelphus coronarius		White Syringa, or mock Orange c	1580
dianthiflorus		Syringa with double Flowers	
nanus	1727	Syringa, the Minor sort	
variegatus	1727	Syringa with stripe'd Leaves	
Phillyrea angustifolia		Phillyrea with very narrow	
rosmarinifolia		Leaves	1597
Phillyrea latifolia		Phillyrea *vera* with broad	
		Leaves	1597
(maculata)		ditto with bloatched Leaves	
buxifolia		ditto with Olive or Box Leaves	1597
ilicifolia		ditto with narrow jagged	
		Leaves	
Phlomis fruticosa		Phlomis, or yellow Bastard	
		Sage Tree	1596

Phylica ericoides	1730	African white-flower'd Heath (T)	'1731'
Physocarpus opulifolius	1727	Spiraea of Virginia, grows large	1690
Picea abies		Firr, called the Spruce Firr	?
? *Picea glauca*		Norway Firr *Pinus sylvestris foliis brevibus Glaucis, comis [sic] parvis albentibus*	1700
Pinus palustris	1727	Pine of Virginia, the Swamp-Pine	'1730'
Pinus pinaster		Pineaster, or wild Pine; the greatest Timber-Tree	1596
Pinus pinea		Pine-Tree, or the large Stone-Pine	c 1500
Pinus strobus		Firr, called the Lord Weymouth's Firr, a five leaved Pine	1705
Pinus sylvestris		Firr, called the Scotch Firr, a sort of Pine; a Timber-Tree	——
Pistacia lentiscus		Lentiscus, or mastich Tree (T)	1632
Pistacia vera		Pistachia from Virginia *Terebinthus Indica Theophrasti, Pistachia Diascorides* (T)	1570

(The description 'from Virginia' must be a misunderstanding by Furber, as Miller's Latin nomenclature is that of the true Pistachio from the Levant)

Platanus x hispanica (x *acerifolia*)		Plane Tree with Maple Leaves, or Spanish Plane Tree	? 1663
Platanus occidentalis		Plane tree occidental; broad-leave'd	1638
Platanus orientalis		Plane Tree oriental; jagged-leave'd	? c 1350
Poinciana — see *Caesalpinia*			
Populus alba		Abele-Tree	
? *globosa*	1727	the English spreading sort	
(*variegata*)	1727	ditto, with stripe'd Leaves	
? *Populus canescens*	1727	Abele, the Dutch spiring high	
Populus nigra	1727	Poplar, the Female, or Cotton-Tree	
Populus tremula		Aspen-Tree	——
	1727	Aspen, the white Branched sort	
erecta	1727	ditto, the upright Black sort	
Potentilla fruticosa	1727	Cinquefoile-Tree with yellow Flowers	——
Prunus armeniaca	1727	Apricock-Tree, with bloached Leaves	c 1542
Prunus avium		Cherry-Tree	——
(*variegata*)	1727	ditto, with strip'd Leaves	
flore pleno		Cherry-Tree with double Flowers	
Prunus cerasifera		Mirabolan Plum; blossoms early	1629
Prunus communis (dulcis)		Almond-Tree with white flowers	?

	1727	ditto the sweet, or tender Nuts	
	1727	ditto, with Peach-blossoms	
Prunus domestica		Christmass Plum, or Winter Crack	?
	1727	Plumb, holds its Fruit till Christmass	
	1727	ditto, with yellowish Bloom, from Hanover	
	1727	ditto, the Pruen, from Italy	
	1727	ditto, the Mussel, stripe'd	
	1727	ditto, the Perdrigon, stripe'd	
flore pleno	1727	ditto, with double Bloom	
Prunus glandulosa roseo-plena		Almond-Tree (dwarf) with peach coloured leaves, or double flowering Almond *Persica Africana, nana, flore incarnato plena*	1673
Prunus laurocerasus		Common Laurel	(1611)
variegata		Laurel with strip'd Leaves	
	1727	ditto with white stripe'd Leaves	
	1727	ditto with yellow stripe'd Leaves	
Prunus mahaleb		Machaleb, or perfumed Cherry	1714
?*Prunus maritima*		Cherry Plum of Virginia	(1760)
		Cerasus vel prunus Virginiana	

(Formerly stated to have been introduced in 1818, but now traced back with certainty to before 1760; it seems probable that the original introduction was earlier still)

Prunus padus		Bird Cherry	——
Prunus persica	1727	Nectarine, the Hermaphrodite	?
roseo-plena		Peach Tree with double Flowers	?
Prunus tenella		Dwarf Almond with single Flowers	1683
Prunus virginiana		Cornish, or Cluster Cherry	1724
Ptelea trifoliata	1727	Trefoilator, a new flowering Shrub	1724
Punica granatum		Fruit-bearing Pomegranate Tree (T)	c 1300
flore pleno		Pomegranate Tree with double Flowers (T)	
nana	1727	ditto, the Dwarf, flowering (T)	(1717)
Pyracantha coccinea	1727	Pyracantha, or ever-green Thorn	1629
Pyrus communis flore pleno		Pear Tree with double Flowers	——
	1727	ditto, flowering at Christmass	
foliis variegatis		ditto with stripe'd Leaves	
Quercus alba		White Oak, or Iron Oak	1724
Quercus borealis maxima (rubra)		Broad leaved Oak from Carolina	1724
Quercus coccifera	1727	Kermes Oak, bearing scarlet Grains	1683
Quercus ilex		Ever-green Oak	1581

	1727	Ilex, with long smooth Leaves	
	1727	ditto, with round smooth Leaves	
Quercus nigra		Water Oak from Carolina	1723
Quercus phellos		Willow leaved Oak from New England	1723
?Quercus pseudosuber Santi	1727	Cork, the Bastard White of Genoua	
Quercus robur		Oak Tree	——
variegata		ditto with strip'd Leaves	
Quercus suber		Cork Tree (T)	1677
	1727	ditto, the true Ever-green	
Quercus virginiana		Ilex, the Minor, from Carolina	(1727)
Rhamnus alaternus		Alaternus with round leaves	1629
angustifolia		ditto, with narrow leaves	
variegata		ditto, with silver edged leaves	
foliis aureis		ditto, with golden edged leaves	
foliis maculatis		ditto, with bloached leaves	
	1727	ditto, the Dutch Gold-edged	
	1727	ditto, with Rosemary Leaves	
	1727	ditto, the Broad shining leav'd	
	1727	ditto, the Broad-leav'd, saw'd Edges	
Rhamnus cathartica	1727	Buckthorn, the English sort	——
Rhamnus frangula	1727	Alder, the Black Mountain, or Franguilea	——
Rhus cotinus (Cotinus coggygria)		Coccigria	1629
Rhus glabra		Virginian Sumach	1620
Rhus radicans		Poison Tree of Virginia two Sorts (1)	1632
Rhus toxicodendron		Poison Tree of Virginia (2)	1640
Rhus typhina	1727	Buckshorn, with Velvet Branches	1629
	1727	ditto, with smooth Branches	
Ribes alpinum	1727	Curran-Tree, with Gooseberry Leaves	
(variegata)	1727	Curran, with Gooseberry Leaves striped	
Ribes oxyacanthoides	1727	Curran, from Pensylvania	1705
Ribes grossularia (uva-crispa)	1727	Goosberry, with stripe'd Leaves	——
Ribes nigrum variegatum	1727	Curran, the Black, with stripe'd Leaves	——
Ribes sativum variegatum	1727	Curran, the Red, with stripe'd Leaves	——
Robinia pseudoacacia		Acacia of Virginia	?1634
Rosa x alba		Common white Rose Blush; Maiden's Blush	
Rosa centifolia		Single Province Rose	

		Cabbage Province Rose
		Dutch Province Rose
		Red Province Rose
		Dutch hundred-leaved Rose
muscosa		Moss Province Rose
Rosa cinnamomea (majalis)		Single Cinnamon Rose
plena		Double Cinnamon Rose
Rosa damascena plena		Double Damask Rose
bifera		Monthly Rose
versicolor		York and Lancaster Rose
		Mrs Hart's, or the strip'd Damask Rose
Rosa foetida		Yellow Austrian Rose
bicolor		Red Austrian Rose
Rosa francofurtana		Frankfort Rose
Rosa gallica plena		Double red Rose
vellutinaeflora		Single Velvet Rose
plena		Double Velvet Rose
versicolor		Rosa Mundi
Rosa hemisphaerica		Double yellow Rose
Rosa moschata Herrm.		Single Musk Rose
plena		Double Musk Rose
Rosa pimpinellifolia		The Burnet-leave'd Rose
		Dwarf Scotch Rose, finely stripe'd
Rosa sempervirens		Evergreen Rose
Rosa villosa (pomifera)		The Apple Rose
(other varieties)		Belgick Blush Rose
		Childing Rose
		Marbled Rose
		Dwarf Red Rose
		Virgin Rose; Rose without Thorns
		Single White Rose
		Dwarf White Rose
		Single (Dwarf) Yellow Rose
Rosmarinus officinalis		Rosmary with narrow Leaves c 1340
		ditto with broad Leaves
aureus		ditto with yellow strip'd Leaves
foliis argenteis		ditto with silver strip'd Leaves
Rubus occidentalis	1727	Bramble, the upright, of Virginia 1696
? pallidus	1727	Bramble with white Berries
Rubus odoratus	1727	Rasberry, the flowering of Virginia 1700
Ruscus hypophyllum		
trifoliatus	1727	Russos with Trefoile Leaves c 1625
Salix babylonica	1727	Willow, the Weeping, from Babylon 1692
Salix pentandra		Laurel leav'd, or Dutch Willow ——
Sambucus nigra		

albo-variegata	1727	Elder, the common variegated	
laciniata	1727	ditto, with Parsley-like Leaves	
viridis	1727	ditto, with greenish white Berries	
alba	1727	ditto, with crystal white Berries	
Sassafras albidum		Sassafras Tree; from Virginia	1633
Satureia thymbra	1730	Tree Savory (T)	1640
Solanum dulcamara		Amara dulcis, or Bitter Sweet with white Flowers	—
variegatum		with strip'd leaves	
Solanum pseudocapsicum	1727	Amomum Plinij, or Winter-Cherry	1596
Sorbus aria		Wild Service with white Leaves	—
	1727	Aria, or wild Service-Tree; Service, Aria Theophrasti	
Sorbus aucuparia		Wild Ash, or Quick Beam; the wild Service Tree with Ash Leaves	—
	1727	Ash, the Mountain, or quick Beam	
(variegata)		ditto, with striped Leaves	
Sorbus domestica		True Service Tree with Ashen Leaves	—
Sorbus torminalis		Common wild Service Tree	—
	1727	Service, the true English sort	
Spartium junceum		Spanish Broom	1548
Spielmannia — see *Oftia*			
Spiraea hypericifolia	1727	Hypericum Frutex, a Shrub	1640
Spiraea salicifolia		Spiraea Frutex	1586
Staphylea pinnata		Staphylodendron, or Bladder Nut	1596
Staphylea trifolia		Three leav'd Virginian Bladder Nut; Staphylodendron of Virginia with three Leaves	1640
Sutherlandia frutescens	1730	Scarlet Colutea (T)	1683
?Symphoricarpos orbiculatus	1727	St Peter's Shrub, a low bushy Tree	1727
Syringa x persica		Persian Lilac with whole Leaves	1634
laciniata		ditto, with cut Leaves	1650
Syringa vulgaris		Lilac with purple Flowers	c 1580
		ditto, with white Flowers Blue Lilac	
(alba variegata)	1727	Lilac, the white, with stripe'd Leaves	
Tamarix gallica		Tree Tamarisk, or French Tamarisk	—
Taxodium distichum	1727	Cypress, the American, sheds its Leaves	1640
Taxus baccata		Common Yew	—
nana		Dwarf Yew	
variegata		Yew with variegated Leaves	

Latin name	Date	English name	Date
Teucrium fruticans		Spanish Tree Germander (T)	1633
Thuja occidentalis		Arbor Vitae	1596
variegata		ditto, with strip'd leaves	
Tilia cordata		Lime Tree with small Leaves	——
Tilia platyphyllos		Lime Tree with large Leaves	——
corallina		ditto, with red Twigs; the Russian with red Twigs	
	1727	ditto with black Twigs	
	1727	ditto, the Russian, with green Twigs	
Ulmus glabra		Broad leav'd rough Elm, or Wych Hazel	——
variegata		Wych Elm with strip'd Leaves	
fastigiata	1727	Elm, the Devonshire, narrow-leav'd, upright	

(other varieties named in 1727: the Essex, with spreading Branches; the narrow-leave'd upright; white-bark'd and large-leave'd; the French, large-leave'd)

Latin name	Date	English name	Date
Ulmus x hollandica major		Dutch Elm	c 1680
	1727	Elm, the Dutch, large-leave'd spreading	
variegata	1727	ditto, with variegated Leaves	
Ulmus procera		Common Elm Tree	——
variegata		the English, with stripe'd Leaves	
		British Elm, a seedling with exceeding broad Leaves, and a very free Shooter	
		Hertfordshire Elm, spreading	
		Petworth Elm, large-leave'd spreading	
Viburnum laevigatum		Cassine, or Cashioberry Bush from Carolina	1724
Viburnum lantana		Viburnum, Wayfaring Tree, or Plant, mealy Tree	——
variegatum		ditto, with strip'd Leaves	
Viburnum opulus		Gelder Rose; Gelder Rose or Elder Rose with flat Flowers	——
sterile		ditto with round Flowers	
(variegatum)		Strip'd Gelder Rose, or Water Elder	
Viburnum prunifolium	1727	Hawthorn of Virginia, black fruit	(1717)
Viburnum tinus		Laurustinus, with rough Leaves	1560
variegatum	1727	the rough leav'd, stripe'd	
lucidum	1727	ditto, with shining Leaves (T)	
	1727	with long shining Leaves	
	1727	with round shining Leaves	
		ditto, with small Leaves, hardy	
		Bastards shining leaved (T)	
	1727	the shining-leav'd, stripe'd (T)	

Vinca major		Broad leav'd Perewincle	?
Vinca minor		Narrow leav'd Periwincle	——
alba		with white Flowers	
	1727	with white Flowers, stripe'd	
caeruleo-plena		Double flowering Periwincle	
variegata		Yellow strip'd Periwincle	
argenteo-variegata		Silver strip'd Periwincle	
Vitex agnus-castus		Agnus Castus or Chaste Tree	1570
latifolia	1727	ditto, with broad Leaves	1570
Vitis vinifera var.	1727	Vine, with stripe'd Leaves	
Wisteria frutescens	1730	Carolina kidney bean tree	1724
Zizyphus jujuba	1730	Zisolo from Genoa (T)	1633

Herbaceous perennials and bulbs

Achillea ageratum	1730	Double white Maudlin	1570
Aeonium arboreum		Sedums five Sorts (1) (T)	1640
	1730	Tree Sedum	
Aeonium canariense		Sedums five Sorts (2) (T)	1699
Agrostemma — see *Lychnis*			
Althaea (Alcea) rosea		Hollyhocks, or Garden Mallows,	
		several Sorts	? c 1275
	1730	Scarlet; White; Double	
Amaryllis belladonna	1730	Belladona Lilly (T)	1712
Anaphalis margaritacea		Eternal, White	1596
		(see also *Helichrysum*)	
Anemone coronaria		Anemonies, several Sorts	1596

(also including varieties of *A. hortensis* and *A. pavonina;* in 1730 Furber
illustrated 20 kinds including single blue, Persian blue, purple, purple &
white, purple striped, dark red, rose, scarlet, and striped, as well as named
sorts). See also *Hepatica, Pulsatilla*.

Anthemis nobilis plena	1730	Camomile, double	——
Anthericum liliago		Spiderwort, three Sorts (1)	1596
		(see also *Paradisea, Tradescantia)*	
Apios tuberosa	1727	Apios of America, a Climber	1640
Apocynum venetum	1730	Willow-leav'd Apocynum	1690
Aquilegia canadensis	1730	Virginian Columbine	1640
Aquilegia vulgaris var.	1730	Columbine strip'd	——
?*Arctotis aspera*	1730	Cape Marigold (T)	1710
Aristolochia pistolochia		A Sort of Birthwort, falsely	
		called the Snake-root *Aristo-*	
		lochia Pistolochia dicta	1597
?*Aristolochia serpentaria*	1730	Virginian Birthwort	1632

(Furber may have discarded *A. pistolochia* in favour of this genuinely
American species, but this entry cannot be regarded as certain)

Armeria maritima		Thrift, three Sorts (1) Red;	——
		(2) White	——
?*Armeria montana*		Thrift, three Sorts (3)	——
Asphodeline lutea		Asphodils, two Sorts (2)	1596
	1730	Yellow Asphodil	
		(see also *Asphodelus)*	
Asphodelus albus		Asphodils, two Sorts (1)	1596

	1730	White Asphodil	
		(see also *Asphodeline*)	
Asphodelus fistulosus	1730	Dwarf white King Spear	1596
Aster carolinianus	1730	Carolina Star flower	?
Aster grandiflorus	1730	Virginian Aster	1720
?*Aster novae-belgii*	1730	Michaelmas Daisie	1710
?*Aster paniculatus*	1730	Spiked Aster	1640
Bellis perennis		Daisies, several Sorts	—
Campanula spp.		Campanula's, several Sorts	

(These would certainly have included *C. persicifolia*, 1596, *C. persicifolia alba* and their double forms, and *C. pyramidalis* 1594).

Campanula trachelium plena	1730	Double blew Throatwort	—
alba plena	1730	Double white Throatwort	—
Canarina campanula	1730	Canary Campanula (T)	1696
Canna indica	1730	Scarlet Indian Cane (T)	1570
Canna lutea	1730	Yellow Indian Cane (T)	1629
Cardamine pratensis flore pleno	1730	Double Cuckow Flower	—
Centranthus — see *Kentranthus*			
Chenopodium capitatum		Strawberry-spinage	
Chenopodium multifidum	1727	Stone-Crop-Tree	'1732'
Chrysanthemum leucanthemum	1730	White Corn Marigold	—
Chrysanthemum parthenium			
flore pleno	1730	Double Featherfew	—
Clematis integrifolia	1730	Hungarian Climer	1573
Clematis recta		Flammula Jovis	1597
Colchicum spp.		Colchicums double and single, many Sorts	

(In 1730 these certainly included *C. agrippinum*, *C. autumnale* with white form and double, double white and double striped)

Convallaria majalis		Lilies of the Valley, two Sorts	—
	1730	White	
rosea	1730	Blush red	
?*Coreopsis auriculata*	1730	Marigold tree	1699
'Cotyledon'		Cotyledons four Sorts	
(see *Cotyledon, Crassula, Rochea*)			
Cotyledon oblonga		Cotyledons four Sorts (1) (T)	1690
Crassula perfoliata		Cotyledons four Sorts (2) (T)	1700
Crassula tetragona		Cotyledons four Sorts (3) (T)	1711
Crocus spp.		Crocus's, several Sorts	

(These would have included forms of *C. aureus, C. vernus, C. sativus, C. serotinus,* and *C. susianus*)

	1730	White	
	1730	Small Yellow	
	1730	Great blew	
	1730	Small blew	
	1730	Yellow Dutch	
	1730	Small white strip'd	
Cyclamen spp.		Cyclamens, two Sorts	

(In 1724 these were probably *C. neapolitanum* and its white variety)

?*Cyclamen orbiculatum coum*	1730	Red Spring Cyclamen	1596
?*album*	1730	White Cyclamen	
Cyclamen neapolitanum	1730	Red Sow Bread	1583
album	1730	White Sow Bread	

?*Cyclamen persicum*	1730	Spring Cyclamen white Edg'd	
Cypripedium calceolus	1730	Ladies Slipper	——
Dianthus caryophyllus		Carnations, several Sorts that	
		blow without breaking the Pod	c 1475
Dianthus plumarius		Pinks single and double,	
		several Sorts	1629
Dictamnus albus (fraxinella)		Fraxinella, two Sorts	1596
		White	
purpureus		Red	
Endymion — see *Scilla*			
Eranthis hyemalis		Winter Aconites	1596
Erythronium dens-canis		Dens canis, two Sorts	1596
	1730	Blush Red	
album	1730	White	
'Eternal' — see *Anaphalis, Helichrysum*			
Euphorbia amygdaloides			
variegata	1730	Strip'd Spurge	——
Fritillaria imperialis		Crown Imperials, several Sorts	1590
(maxima lutea		Yellow	
maxima rubra		Red	
variegata		Striped-leaved)	
Fritillaria meleagris		Frittillaria's, several Sorts	?

(The varieties available included the Chequered, White, Dark purple and Brown forms)

Galanthus nivalis		Snow-drops, double and single	?
Gentiana acaulis		Gentianella	1596
Geranium macrorrhizum	1730	Great Purple Cranes bill	1576
Geranium phaeum	1730	Black Cranes bill	?
Geranium sanguineum	1730	Scarlet Cranes bill	——
?*Geranium striatum*	1730	Embroider'd Cranes bill	1629
Geum montanum	1730	Mountain Avens	1597
Helianthus decapetalus	1730	Perennial dwarf Sunflower	1597
?*Helichrysum orientale*		Eternal, Yellow spik'd	1629
Helichrysum stoechas		Eternal, Yellow round	1629
		(see also *Anaphalis)*	
Helleborus niger	1730	Christmas Flower	?
Helleborus viridis	1730	Lesser black Hellebore	——
Hemerocallis flava		Yellow Day Lily	1570
Hepatica triloba (Anemone			
hepatica)		Hepatica's, single and double	1573
Hieracium pilosella form	1730	Double Mouse ear	——
Hyacinthus orientalis		Hyacinths double and single,	
		many Sorts	1596
Iris spp.		Iris's with tuberose Roots,	
		several Sorts	

(The species would have included *I. florentina, I. germanica, I. pallida* and *I. variegata)*

Iris chamaeiris ⎤			
Iris pumila ⎦	1730	Dwarf striped Iris	1596
?*Iris versicolor*	1730	Narrow-leaved striped Iris	'1732'
		Iris's with bulbose Roots,	
		several Sorts	

Iris persica	1730	Persian Iris	1629
Iris xiphioides	1730	Iris major, Ultramarine and	
		Prussian blue	1570
Iris xiphium			1596
Kentranthus (Centranthus)			
ruber	1730	Broad leav'd red Valerian	——
albus	1730	White Valerian	
Kniphofia uvaria	1730	Iris uvaria	1707
Lathyrus vernus	1730	Venetian Vetch; True ditto	1629
Lilium bulbiferum croceum			
flore pleno		Double orange Lily	1596
Lilium candidum		Lilies, double and single	?
plenum		(Double)	
purpureum	1730	White Lilly strip'd with purple	
Lilium spp.		Martagons, several Sorts	
Lilium chalcedonicum	1730	Scarlet Martagon	1596
Lilium martagon flore pleno	1730	Double Martagon	1596
Lilium superbum	1730	Virginian Scarlet Martagon	1727
Lilium pyrenaicum	1730	Yellow Martagon	1596
rubrum	1730		1596
Lilium pomponium		Red Martagon	1629
Linaria purpurea	1730	Purple toad flax	1648
Lobelia cardinalis	1730	Broad leav'd Cardinal (T)	1629
Lotus corniculatus	1730	Lotus with yellow flowers	——
Lychnis chalcedonica		Lychnis's three Sorts, single and double (Presumably the three colour varieties, scarlet, flesh-coloured and white)	1596
rubra plena	1730	Double scarlet Mountain Lychnis	
Lychnis (Agrostemma) coronaria		Rose Campions, double and single	1596
Lychnis flos-cuculi pleniflora		Double ragged Robin	——
Malva alcea	1730	Purple Mallow	1597
Melandrium (Silene) album	1730		
multiplex		White Batchelors Button	——
Mesembryanthemum spp.		Ficoides twelve sorts	

(Some 40 species of Mesembryanthemum had been introduced before 1724, including *M. barbatum* 1705, *M. coccineum* 1696, *M. expansum* 1705, *M. floribundum* 1704, *M. hispidum* 1704, *M. subhispidum* 1704, *M. tenuifolium* 1700, *M. tripolium* 1700, and *M. tuberosum* 1705; besides the four below)

?*Mesembryanthemum edule*	1730	Ficoides or Fig Marigold	1690
?*Mesembryanthemum glaucum*	1730	Triangle Yellow Ficoides	1696
?*Mesembryanthemum latum*	1730	Yellow Ficoides	1620
Mesembryanthemum micans	1730	Purple Ficoides	1704
Mirabilis jalapa	1730	Yellow strip'd Marvel of Peru (T)	1596
Muscari botryoides album	1730	White Grape flower	1596
Narcissus spp.		Narcissus's, several Sorts	

(At least a half-dozen species and many varieties had been in trade long before 1724, notably *N. bulbocodium, N. hispanicus, N. x incomparabilis, N. odorus, N. poeticus,* and *N. pseudonarcissus* with varieties)

Narcissus jonquilla		Jonquils, double and single	1596
Nerine sarniensis	1730	Guernsey Lilly (T)	1659
Omphalodes verna	1730	Creeping Borage or Bugloss	1633

Ophrys apifera	1730	Orchis or Bee flower	—
Papaver nudicaule	1730	Yellow perennial Poppy	'1730'
Papaver orientale		Perennial Poppy	1714
Paradisea liliastrum		Spiderwort, three Sorts (2)	1629
		(see also *Anthericum,*	
		Tradescantia)	
Pelargonium acetosum	1730	Sour-leav'd Geranium (T)	1710
Pelargonium inquinans	1730	Scarlet Geranium (T)	1714
?*Pelargonium papilionaceum*	1730	Best flowering Geranium (T)	1724
Pelargonium zonale marginatum	1730	Strip'd leav'd Geranium (T)	1710
Pelargonium spp.		Geraniums, several Sorts with	
		knobbed Roots	

(Tuberous-rooted species introduced before 1724 included *P. gibbosum* 1712, *P. lobatum* 1710, *P. myrrhifolium* 1696, and *P. triste* 1631)

Phytolacca americana	1730	Virginian Poke	1615
Polemonium coeruleum	1730	Greek Valerian	—
Polianthes tuberosa	1730	Tuberose (T)	1629
Primula auricula		Auricula's, several Sorts	1596

(In 1730 Furber illustrated 15 named varieties)

Primula x variabilis		Polyanthos, several Sorts	

(In 1730 Furber illustrated seven different kinds)

Primula vulgaris	1730	Winter white Primrose	—
Pulmonaria officinalis	1730	Jerusalem Cowslip	1597
Pulsatilla vulgaris			
(*Anemone pulsatilla)*	1730	Blew Passe flower	—
	1730	White Passe flower	
Ranunculus aconitifolius		Mountain Ranunculus's	1596
Ranunculus asiaticus		Ranunculus's, several Sorts	1596
Ranunculus ficaria plena	1730	Double Pilewort	—
Rochea coccinea		Cotyledons four Sorts (4) (T)	1710

(This is probably what is illustrated in 1730, no. 19 in January, as 'Dwarf Tithymall')

Saponaria officinalis albo-plena	1730	Double white Soapwort	—
Saxifraga granulata plena		Double Saxifrage	—
Scilla amoena	1730	Winter blew Hyacinth	1596
Scilla bifolia	1730	Dwarf blew starry Hyacinth	—
alba	1730	Dwarf white starry Hyacinth	
Scilla (Endymion) hispanica	1730	Blew-bell Hyacinth	1683
Scilla italica	1730	Larger blew starry Hyacinth	1605
Scilla peruviana		Hyacinths of Peru, two Sorts	1607
(alba		White variety)	
'Sedum' (see *Aeonium, Sedum,*			
Sempervivum)		Sedums five Sorts	
Sedum cepaea		Sedums five Sorts (3)	1640
Sedum stellatum		Sedums five Sorts (4)	1640
Sempervivum arachnoideum		Sedums five Sorts (5)	1699
	1730	The Cobweb or red Sedum	
Silene — see *Melandrium*			
?*Solidago altissima*	1730	Golden Rod	1686
Solidago canadensis	1730	Golden Rod	1648
Sternbergia lutea	1730	Yellow Colchicum	1596
Trachelium caeruleum	1730	Pona's blew Throatwort	1640
Tradescantia virginiana		Spiderwort, three Sorts (3)	1629

flore pleno	1730	Double Virginian Silk-Grass	
Trollius europaeus	1730	Yellow Globe Flower	——
Tulipa gesneriana		Tulips double and single many Sorts	1577
(In 1730 Furber illustrated ten varieties)			
Viola odorata		Violets, several Sorts	——
Viola tricolor	1730	Pansy or Hearts Ease	——
Zygophyllum fabago	1730	Bean Caper	1586

Annuals and biennials
Biennials are marked B.

Abutilon — see *Sida*			
Adonis aestivalis	1730	Pheasants Eye (two sorts) (1)	1629
Adonis autumnalis	1730	Pheasants Eye (2)	——
??*Amaranthus melancholicus*			
tricolor	1730	Amaranthus trachee	1548
Anacyclus pyrethrum	1730	Pellitory with Daisy flowers	1570
Anacyclus valentinus	1730	Great Spanish Ox Eye	1656
Antirrhinum majus variegatum		Strip'd Snapdragon (B)	c 1500
Basella rubra	1730	Basella (T)	1688
Borago officinalis	1730	Borage	? c 1200
Campanula medium		Campanula's, several Sorts (B)	1597
Celosia cristata	1730	Purple Coxcomb Amaranth (T)	1570
aurea	1730	Yellow Amaranth (T)	
coccinea	1730	All Red Amaranth (T)	
?*Centaurea cyanus*		Batchellors Buttons, two Sorts (see also *Melandrium*)	
	1730	Blue Cornflower	——
Centaurea moschata purpurea	1730	Purple Sultan	1629
Cheiranthus cheiri		Wall Flowers, many Sorts (B)	? c 1275
Chrysanthemum segetum	1730	Yellow Corn Marigold	
Delphinium ajacis	1730	Double blew Larkspur	1573
Dianthus barbatus		Double and single Sweet Williams (B)	1573
x var.		Fairchild's Mule (or Double rose Sweet William) (B)	
Dimorphotheca pluvialis	1730	Cape Marigold white within (T)	1699
Gomphrena globosa	1730	Purple Amaranthoides (T)	1714
Iberis umbellata	1730	Strip'd Candy tuft	1596
Impatiens balsamina	1730	Double, Single strip'd Female Balsam (T)	1596
Ipomoea — see *Pharbitis*			
Lathyrus odoratus	1730	Purple Sweet Pea	1700
Lupinus albus	1730	White Lupin	c 1300
Matthiola incana	1730	Double Stock (B)	? c 1300
Mimosa pudica	1730	Humble Plant (T)	1638
Nicotiana tabacum	1730	Indian Tobacco	1570
Nigella damascena	1730	Blew Nigella or Fennel Flower	1570
?*Oenothera fruticosa*	1730	New Tree Primrose (B)	'1737'
Pharbitis (Ipomoea) purpurea	1730	Purple Convolvulus	1629
Polygonum orientale	1730	Oriental Arssmart	1707
Ricinus communis	1730	Palma Christi	1548

Scabiosa atropurpurea	1730	Musk Scabious	1629
Sida abutilon (Abutilon			
avicennae)	1730	Yellow Ketmia (T)	1596
Silene armeria flore pleno		Double Lychnis, a Sort of	
		Catch-Fly; Double Catch-fly	——
Tagetes erecta	1730	African Marigold (T)	1596
var.	1730	Quill'd African Marigold	
Tagetes patula	1730	French Marigold (T)	1573
Tropaeolum majus	1730	Single Nasturtium	1686
plenum	1730	Double Nasturtium	
Valerianella coronata	1730	Valerianella	'1731'
Verbascum lychnitis	1730	White flower Moth Mullein (B)	——

Many of the plants in Furber's lists had attracted attention at earlier dates, as well as several not here listed: in 1717 the annual *Convolvulus tricolor;* two years later the biennial *Digitalis ferruginea;* in 1720 Strawberry-Spinage *(Chenopodium capitatum)* and the Carnation Rose for which Furber was charging the high price of 12 shillings. In 1721 he had the Amber Tree *(Anthospermum aethiopicum)* and a 'Mespylus', possibly *Amelanchier ovalis,* at 10 shillings, with Yellow Sultans *(Centaurea moschata)* among the annuals. (See Michael McGarvie and John H. Harvey in *Garden History,* XI, 1 [1982] 6-36.)

Appendix 2: Roses in cultivation in Britain before 1830

My special thanks go to Mrs Hazel Le Rougetel for kindly checking the list for availability and for much other help and information. For the current availability of roses see *Find that Rose,* compiled annually by the Rose Growers Association, 303 Mile End Road, Colchester, Essex CO4 5EA.

Dates in brackets are those of introduction or earliest cultivation; if expressed thus (-1800), the date is known to be earlier than that given, but uncertain. Where no date is given the species is either native or is believed to have been here in the middle ages (before 1540).

Climbing and rambling roses are noted: apart from native briers, notably *Rosa arvensis* and *R. canina,* there were no climbing roses in effective cultivation before about 1800, with the single exception of the true Musk Rose, *R. moschata* Herrm., also notable as the only late-flowering species, from July to October. 'Climber' indicates a rose with stiff stems; 'Rambler' one of lax habit easy to train but requiring support.

Rosa
'Adélaîde d'Orléans' (1826)   Rambler
'Agatha' (-1820)
'Aimée Vibert' (1828)   Climber
x *alba* 'White Rose'
'Alba Maxima' (-1600)
'Alba Semiplena' (-1550)
    'Alpine' — see *pendulina*
    altaica — see *pimpinellifolia altaica*
'Amadis' (1829)   Rambler
    'Apothecary's Rose' — see *gallica officinalis*
    'Apple Rose' — see *villosa*
arvensis   Rambler
'Assemblage des Beautés' (1790)
    'Austrian Copper' — see *foetida bicolor*
    'Austrian Yellow' — see *foetida*
banksiae (1807)   Rambler (T)
banksiae lutea (-1824)   Rambler (T)
banksiae normalis (1796)   Rambler (T)
    biebersteinii — see *horrida*
blanda (1773)
'Blush Damask' (1780)
'Blush Noisette' (-1817)
    'Boursault Rose' — see *lheritierana*
bracteata (1795) 'Macartney'   Rambler (T)
brunonii (1822) 'Himalayan Musk Rose'   Rambler
    bullata — see *centifolia bullata*
    'Burnet Double White', / '...Pink' — see *pimpinellifolia*
    'Burr Rose' — see *roxburghii*
    'Cabbage Rose' — see *centifolia*
canina 'Dog Rose'   Climber
carolina (1726)

'Celestial' (-1800)
celsiana (-1750)
centifolia (-1596) 'Cabbage Rose', 'Provence Rose'
centifolia bullata (1801) 'Lettuce-leaved Rose'
centifolia cristata (1826) 'Chapeau de Napoléon'
centifolia muscosa (1724) 'Old Pink Moss'
centifolia parvifolia (-1770) 'Pompon de Bourgogne'
'Champneys' Pink Cluster' (1811) Rambler
　'Chapeau de Napoléon' — see *centifolia cristata*
　'Cherokee Rose' — see *laevigata*
chinensis — see 'Old Blush China'
cinnamomea (majalis) (-1600)
　'Cumberland' — see *gallica violacea*
damascena bifera (? -1600) 'Quatre Saisons'
damascena trigintipetala (? c 1520) 'Kazanlik'
damascena versicolor (-1629) 'York & Lancaster'
'De Meaux' (? 1770) 'Rose de Meaux'
　'De Redouté' — see *prolifera* 'de Redouté'
'Desprez à Fleurs Jaunes' (? 1826) Climber
　'Dog Rose' — see *canina*
'Duchess of Portland' (? 1800) 'Portland Rose'
　(Note: this may not be identical with the 'Portland Rose' in trade by 1782)
x *dupontii* (-1817)
'Du Roi' (1815)
'Du Roi à Fleurs Pourpres' (1819)
　'Dwarf Labrador' — see *nitida*
eglanteria (rubiginosa) 'Sweet Brier'
eglanteria 'Manning's Blush' (-1826)
'Empress Josephine' (c 1810)
　(Note: not the ancient *Rosa francofurtana*, of which it is an improved form)
'Félicité et Perpétue' (1827) Rambler
　'Ferox' — see *horrida*
foetida (-1590) 'Austrian Yellow'
foetida bicolor (-1590) 'Austrian Copper'
　'French Rose' — see *gallica*
gallica 'French Rose', 'Red Rose'
gallica officinalis 'Apothecary's Rose'
gallica vellutinaeflora (? -1597) 'Single Velvet'
gallica versicolor (-1596) 'Rosa Mundi'
gallica violacea (-1803) 'Cumberland', 'La Belle Sultane', 'Semi-double Velvet'
　(Note: a semi-double 'Velvet' rose had been in trade before 1750)
'Gloire de France' (? 1819)
　glutinosa — see *pulverulenta*
hemisphaerica (-1625) 'Sulphur Rose' (T)
x *hibernica* (1795)
　'Himalayan Musk Rose' — see *brunonii*
horrida (biebersteinii) (1796) 'Ferox'
　'Hume's Blush China' — see *odorata*
'Ipsilanté' (1821)
'Jeanne d'Arc' (1818)
　'Kazanlik' — see *damascena trigintipetala*
'Königin von Dänemark' (1820)
　'La Belle Sultane' — see *gallica violacea*

laevigata (c 1794) 'Cherokee Rose'   Rambler (T)
'Lettuce-leaved Rose' — see *centifolia bullata*
lheritierana (1821) 'Boursault Rose' Climber
'Macartney' — see *bracteata*
'Maiden's Blush, Great' (-1500)
'Maiden's Blush, Small' (1797)
   majalis — see *cinnamomea*
'Manning's Blush' — see *eglanteria* 'Manning's Blush'
'Marie Louise' (1813)
moschata Herrm. (-1590)   Climber
multiflora (1810)   Rambler
multiflora carnea (1804)   Rambler
multiflora platyphylla (1816) 'Seven Sisters'   Rambler
nitida (1807) 'Dwarf Labrador'
odorata (-1810) 'Hume's Blush China'
'Old Blush China' (1770) *chinensis*
'Old Pink Moss' — see *centifolia muscosa*
'Ombrée Parfaite' (1823)
'Parks' Yellow China' (1823)
pendulina (1683) 'Alpine'
'Petite Lisette' (1817)
pimpinellifolia (spinosissima)
pimpinellifolia altaica (altaica) (1818)
pimpinellifolia 'Burnet Double Pink', / '... White' (-1650)
pimpinellifolia lutea (-1771) 'Yellow Scotch'
   pomifera — see *villosa*
'Pompon de Bourgogne' — see *centifolia parvifolia*
'Portland Rose' — see 'Duchess of Portland'
'Prairie Rose' — see *setigera*
prolifera 'de Redouté' (-1827) 'De Redouté'
'Provence Rose' — see *centifolia*
pulverulenta (glutinosa) (1821)
   'Quatre Saisons' — see *damascena bifera*
   'Red Rose' — see *gallica*
   'Rosa Mundi' — see *gallica versicolor*
   'Rose d'Amour' — see *virginiana plena*
roxburghii (-1814) 'Burr rose'
   rubiginosa — see *eglanteria*
rubrifolia (1814)
ruga (1827)   Climber
setigera (1800) 'Prairie Rose'
'Seven Sisters' — see *multiflora platyphylla*
'Shailer's White Moss' (1788)
   spinosissima — see *pimpinellifolia*
'Spong' (1805)
   'Sulphur Rose' — see *hemisphaerica*
   'Sweet Brier' — see *eglanteria*
'Tuscany' (-1827)
   'Unique' — see 'White Provence'
   'Velvet, Single' — see *gallica vellutinaeflora*
   'Velvet, Semi-double' — see *gallica violacea*
villosa (pomifera) (-1755) 'Apple Rose'
virginiana (-1640; ? 1724)

virginiana plena (-1820) 'Rose d'Amour'
'White Provence' (1775) 'Unique'
  'White Rose' — see x *alba*
  'Yellow Scotch' — see *pimpinellifolia lutea*
  'York & Lancaster' — see *damascena versicolor*

Some gardens to visit

This is a select list and includes only examples governed by strict adherence to period design as well as planting. In a few cases work is still in progress but the property is already well worth a visit. Before making a special journey, intending visitors are advised to confirm dates and times of opening by telephone or by reference to the annual editions of *Historic Houses, Castles and Gardens open to the Public* and *Museums and Galleries in Great Britain and Ireland* (British Leisure Publications, Windsor Court, East Grinstead RH19 1XA).

Christ Church Cathedral, Oxford. The Cloister Garden is usually open daily when the cathedral is open.

The garden, filling the eastern half of the old cloister garth, is a reconstruction of elements typical of 1490-1500, the date of the monastic cloisters, with trellised fence, border, raised beds and carnations in pots on the lawn, designed by Mrs Mavis Batey. Although such gardens were not actually planted within English cloisters in the middle ages, such a garden could have existed elsewhere within the monastic precincts of St Frideswide's.

Claremont Landscape Garden, Esher, Surrey (NT). Open daily.

Extensive remains of the original plantings of several dates in the eighteenth century, cleared and brilliantly restored since 1975. The unique Amphitheatre was made by Bridgeman in 1715-25 and its survival was unknown until clearance had been in progress for some time. Much undergrowth, especially of Rhododendrons, still remains to be cleared but the estate already gives the impression of classical serenity which it was intended to convey.

Erddig, near Wrexham, Clwyd LL13 0YT. Telephone: 0978 355314 (NT). Open spring to autumn daily except Friday.

In spite of long decay and the need, in parts, for total replanting, these gardens give a complete impression of the layout of 1718-32.

Ham House, Ham, Richmond, Surrey TW10 7YS. Telephone: 01-940 1950 (NT). Open daily except Monday.

Admission to the grounds is free but inside the house there is an important exhibit on the history of the gardens. An outstanding example of careful restoration since 1974 of the original layout of 1671-93. There is a formal garden to east of the house, and a Wilderness of hornbeam with vistas and winding paths to south, beyond the great lawns intersected with gravel walks.

Hampton Court Palace, Hampton Court, London. Telephone: 01-977 8441 (EH). Open daily, admission to the gardens free.
    The principal restored feature is the hemicycle of lime trees on the east facing The Long Water, replanted in 1987 after extensive research by David Jacques with the original species, the Common Lime. The famous Maze (admission charge), north of the Palace, is a surviving section of the old Wilderness of c 1690, but has been changed by modern replanting from hornbeam to yew.

Kew Palace, Royal Botanic Gardens, Kew, Richmond, Surrey. The Queen's Garden is open daily.
    This is a formal design by Sir George Taylor as a re-creation of the original garden of c 1631, of which no record exists. The alleys, mount with summerhouse, general layout and planting are all of the period, though the plan of the parterre behind the palace (the Dutch House) is based on a much earlier French design.

Little Moreton Hall, Congleton, Cheshire CW12 4SD (NT). Telephone: 0260 272018. Open April-September, daily except Tuesday; March and October, Saturdays and Sundays only.
    The knot garden behind the great hall is based on a plan by Leonard Meager (1670), with planting of the period; it is a re-creation, as no detailed records of the old gardens exist.

Moseley Old Hall Gardens, Moseley Old Hall Lane, Fordhouses, Wolverhampton WV10 7HY. Telephone: 0902 782808 (NT). Never open on Monday or Tuesday; enquire for other days.
    The gardens are re-creations to the design of Graham Stuart Thomas, but adhere strictly to the plants of 1650. The large parterre, planted with trees, is of low box hedges and gravel as a measure of economy in upkeep. The plan is one used by the Reverend Walter Stonehouse who in 1631-40 cultivated a remarkably wide selection of plant species in the rectory garden of Darfield, Yorkshire.

Mount Edgcumbe Country Park, Cremyll, near Plymouth. Telephone: 0752 822236. Open daily, admission free.
    Restoration of the zigzags and other parts of the landscape has

been in progress for some years. Replanting of the English, French and Italian Gardens began in the season 1987-88 after several years of research by members of the Garden History Society.

Nuneham Park Conference Centre, Nuneham Courtenay, Oxfordshire. Telephone: 086738 551. It is essential to enquire about opening times.

Restoration of the 34 beds of the flower garden of 1772 by the Reverend William Mason for Lord Harcourt has been in progress since 1982. The relatively informal methods of planting shown in Paul Sandby's views are strictly followed, and the species of plants used are the result of detailed research by Mrs Mavis Batey and Richard Bisgrove.

Painshill Park, Portsmouth Road, Cobham, Surrey (off A245). Telephone: 0932 68113. Open Easter to October on Wednesdays. Groups can book tours for Thursday, Saturday or Sunday.

The main features of Charles Hamilton's great landscape were largely planted in 1738-43, and restoration to the highest standards of authenticity has been in progress under the Painshill Park Trust since 1980.

Painswick Rococo Garden, Painswick, Gloucestershire. Telephone: 0452 813204. Open May-September, Wednesday, Thursday, Sunday and Bank Holiday Mondays.

Restoration under Paul Edwards has been in progress since 1984, of the garden as depicted by Thomas Robins in 1748.

Pitmedden, Udney, Aberdeen, Grampian. Telephone: 06513 2445 (NTS). Gardens open daily.

The formal gardens of 1664-75 have been re-created, but are based upon those shown at Holyroodhouse, Edinburgh, in a view of 1647. This is the most notable period garden in Scotland, particularly for the fine display of authentic flowering plants.

Queen Eleanor's Garden, Winchester Castle, Winchester, Hampshire. Open daily, admission free.

So far the only serious attempt, by Dr Sylvia Landsberg, to re-create a garden of the High Middle Ages, in this case a royal *herbarium* in the courtyard to the south of the surviving Great Hall of Henry III. In spite of an extremely confined position, space has been found for all the features of such a private pleasance of royalty, and the plants are those which would have been grown by Queen Eleanor of Provence and her daughter-in-law Queen Eleanor of Castile before 1291. The stone fountain, the bronze falcon which surmounts it, and the wooden seat are closely based on actual remains of the period at Winchester.

Red Lodge, Park Row, Bristol 1. Telephone: 0272 299771 extension 236. The museum is open daily except Sunday. The knot garden is always visible from the museum and can usually be visited on Saturdays in Summer.

The knot garden, behind the Red Lodge Museum of c 1590, is on the site of one of several gardens which formerly belonged to the house. As there are no descriptions this is an exercise in re-creation, correctly placed to be viewed from the upper windows of the house.

Royal Pavilion Gardens, Brighton, East Sussex BN1 1UE. Telephone: 02703 603005. Open daily, admission free.

These gardens are now being restored to their state in 1825, based on John Nash's own plan and other records. Lawns sweep up to the Pavilion and gravelled paths meander between beds and borders planted with the flowers available to Nash. The absence of edgings to beds and borders should be noted.

Studley Royal (with Fountains Abbey), Fountains, Ripon, North Yorkshire HG4 3DZ. Telephone: 076586 333 (NT). Open daily.

Since 1966, when the Studley Royal estate was acquired by the West Riding County Council, there has been extensive restoration of the temples and other architectural monuments, and of the pieces of water and woodland planting, initially under Mr W. T. C. Walker. This policy has continued, under the North Yorkshire County Council from 1974 and by the National Trust since 1983. The original estate (exclusive of Fountains) is noteworthy as the first break with the formal tradition, and for its superb design by the gardener William Fisher in c 1715 for his patron John Aislabie.

The Swiss Garden, Old Warden, near Biggleswade, Bedfordshire. Telephone: 0234 63222 extension 2330. Open March-October, Wednesday, Thursday, Saturday, Sunday and Bank Holiday Mondays.

Many fine old trees, as well as the earthwork landscape, remain from the original planting of 1829-33, as well as the Swiss Cottage and some features, with others of 1876-77. The glazed dome and transept of the Grotto are of 1830. A meticulous restoration of the buildings and planting has been carried out by Bedfordshire County Council since 1976.

The Tradescant Trust, Museum of Garden History, Lambeth, London (at the gates of Lambeth Palace). Telephone: 01-373 4030 (7 to 9 a.m.); 01-261 1891 (11 a.m. to 3 p.m.). Open mid March to mid December daily except Saturday.

The Tradescant Garden is a part of the churchyard of St Mary's, Lambeth (now converted to the museum), containing the tombs of the Tradescant family and of Admiral Bligh, and a re-created formal garden of the mid seventeenth century designed by the Marchioness of Salisbury.

Tudor House Museum, Bugle Street, Southampton, Hampshire. Telephone: 0703 24216. Open daily except Monday, admission free.

The pioneer example of re-creation of an early garden with strictly authentic features and planting of 1600, designed by Dr Sylvia Landsberg and opened to the public in 1982. The overall impression, with rich herbal aromas added to the visual beauty of the plants and the humming of a hive of bees, provides an unforgettable experience.

Weald and Downland Open Air Museum, Singleton, Chichester, West Sussex PO18 0EU. Telephone: 024363 348. Open April-October, daily; November-March, Wednesdays and Sundays only.

'Bayleaf' is a re-erected Kentish yeoman's house of the fifteenth century with its croft, orchard and re-created garden within a wattled fence. The vegetable and herb garden has been designed by Dr Sylvia Landsberg and planting began in the season 1987-88.

Westbury Court Garden, Westbury-on-Severn, Gloucestershire GL14 1PD. Telephone: 045276 461 (NT). Open April-October daily except Monday and Tuesday. Open Bank Holiday Mondays.

The earliest formal water garden to survive in Britain, of the Dutch school and dating from 1696-1705. It was long derelict but fully restored after 1971 following documentary research by Irvine Gray and with the advice of the Garden History Society.

Wroxton Abbey (College), near Banbury, Oxfordshire. Telephone: 029573 551. Grounds only open daily.

Restoration of the cascades and other water features, together with authentic replanting of the landscape under Paul Edwards, have made Wroxton an outstanding example of a great garden of 1735 and later.

Index

Abbreviations: *c* about; *d* died; G gardener; N nurseryman; S seedsman. Page numbers in italic refer to illustrations.

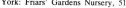